The Only Wine Book You'll Ever Need

By Danny May
With contributions from Andy Sharpe

Adams Media
Avon, MA

Published by Adams Media, an F+W Publications Company
57 Littlefield Street
Avon, MA 02322 USA
www.adamsmedia.com
ISBN 10: 1-59337-101-2
ISBN 13: 978-1-59337-101-2
Printed in Canada.

J   I   H   G   F   E   D   C   B

Library of Congress Cataloging-in-Publication Data
May, Danny.
The only wine book you'll ever need / Danny May ;
with contributions from Andy Sharpe.
p.   cm.
ISBN 1-59337-101-2
1. Wine and wine making. I. Sharpe, Andy. II. Title.
TP548.M4586 2004
641.2'2—dc22
2004004811

Contains portions of material adapted and abridged from *The Everything® Wine Book* by
Danny May and Andy Sharpe, ©1997, Adams Media Corporation.

This publication is designed to provide accurate and authoritative information with
regard to the subject matter covered. It is sold with the understanding that the publisher is not engaged in rendering legal, accounting, or other professional advice. If legal
advice or other expert assistance is required, the services of a competent professional
person should be sought.

—From a *Declaration of Principles* jointly adopted by a
Committee of the American Bar Association and
a Committee of Publishers and Associations

Many of the designations used by manufacturers and sellers to distinguish their products are claimed as trademarks. Where those designations appear in this book and
Adams Media was aware of a trademark claim, the designations have been printed
with initial capital letters.

This book is available at quantity discounts for bulk purchases.
For information, please call 1-800-289-0963.

Visit our home page at *www.adamsmedia.com*.

Contents

Introduction: What Is Wine? vii

Part 1: Wine 101 / 1

Chapter 1: A Brief History of Wine / 3
The Origins of Wine • The Proliferation of Wine in the Ancient World • Winemaking Spreads to the New World • Setbacks in the Prohibition Era • The Wine Boom in America

Chapter 2: Types of Wine / 15
Table Wine (Where Else Would You Put a Wineglass?) • Sparkling Wine, or Bubbly • Dessert Wine • Fortified Wine • Kosher Wine

Chapter 3: How Is Wine Made? / 39
Combating Oxidation • Through the Glass, Clearly • Differences Between White Wine and Red Wine Production

Part 2: Why We Love Wine / 51

Chapter 4: What Makes Good Wine Good? / 53
Wine #1: White Served at 45°–50°F • Wine #2: Red Served at 55°–60°F • The Self-Fulfilling Prophesy of Perfection • Great Grapes • The Final Analysis

Chapter 5: The Quality Spectrum / 61
Category 1: Jug Wines ($10–$13 per 4-Liter Bottle) • Category 2: "Fighting" Varietals ($5–$8) • Category 3: Midrange Varietals ($8–$18) • Category 4: Handcrafted Wines ($18–$30) • Category 5: Reserve Wines ($30 and up) • Vintages • What Makes Expensive Wines Expensive? • Why Expensive Wines Are Worth It

Chapter 6: Wine Flaws / 73
The Wine Is Too Old • The Wine Is Too Young • The Wine Is Carsick • The Wine Is Poorly Made • The Wine Is out of Balance • The Wine Is the Wrong Temperature • The Wine Is "Corked" • The Wine Is Oxidized • The Wine Is "Bretty" • The Wine Is Fizzy • The Wine Is Cloudy • Stuff Has Settled on the Bottom • The Wine Is Too Expensive

Part 3: The Wine Universe / 83

Chapter 7: The Region-Versus-Variety Debate / 85
Old-World Distinctions • New-World Differences • The Current Lay of the Land

Chapter 8: Varietal Wines, Grape by Grape / 89
Red Wine Grapes: Cabernet Sauvignon • Pinot Noir • Merlot • Syrah/ Shiraz • Zinfandel • Nebbiolo • Sangiovese • Grenache • Gamay • Tempranillo • Malbec • Cabernet Franc • Barbera • *White Wine Grapes:* Chardonnay • Sauvignon Blanc • Riesling • Chenin Blanc • Pinot Blanc • Semillon • Viognier • Pinot Grigio/Pinot Gris • Gewürztraminer • Grüner Veltliner

Chapter 9: Wine Regions / 137
The Home of the Vine • France • Italy • Germany • Spain • Portugal • Austria • The United States • Argentina • Chile • South Africa • Australia • New Zealand • The Rest of the World

Part 4: Choosing and Serving Wine / **185**

Chapter 10: The Economics of Wine / 187
Economics 101 • Wine Merchants in the Real World • Supply Side Economics . . . • . . . And Demand • More Economic Theory • Restaurant Wine

Chapter 11: Shopping for Wine / 195
A Guide to Wine Stores • Anatomy of a Wine Store • Wine Distribution in Retail Stores • In the Know • Wine for Entertaining a Crowd • Wine for Small Dinner Parties • "House Wine" for Everyday Sipping • Stocking a Wine Cellar

Chapter 12: Navigating the Restaurant Wine List / 215
Buying Wine in a Restaurant • Wine by the Glass Is Often Very
Expensive • Know the Price Structure • Making a Selection • The
Wine Ritual • How Should You Tip? • Can You Bring Your Own
Bottle (BYOB)? • The Bottom Line

Chapter 13: Wine and Food / 223
Matching Food and Wine • You Don't Always Need to Match •
Good Wine and Food Matches • Enjoying Wine Without Food •
Cooking with Wine

Part 5: Resources / 239

Web Site Reference Guide 241
Bibliography 247
Glossary 249

Index 275

What Is Wine?

WINE IS AN alcoholic beverage, and so much more . . .

Before electricity, before running water, before medical science, there was soothing and delicious wine to gladden the heart, to make life's rigors more bearable, and to make good times even more enjoyable. Throughout its seventy or more centuries at the table of Western civilization, wine has inspired the imaginations of poets, oiled the voices of orators, emboldened the shy, wooed sweethearts-to-be, sealed marriages, marked religious ceremonies, honored births and anniversaries, and christened ships. The same cannot be said of beer or whisky. Unlike the production of beer and spirits, which require relatively complex processes such as malting and distillation, wine is almost a naturally occurring product. Grapes *want* to become wine, and they require minimal processing to do so.

Wine is made from grape juice when the natural grape sugars are transformed into ethyl alcohol through the activity of naturally occurring yeast cells. To a chemist, therefore, wine is a solution of water, alcohol, acids, and the various organic compounds formed during fermentation. Wine is the most acidic drink that passes our lips. The sharp impression made on the mouth by wine acids—tartaric, tannic, malic, and/or lactic—provides the backbone that gives clarity and purpose to a wine's fruity flavors and aromas. It is the acidity in wine that aids digestion and, along with the alcohol, helps to preserve wine in the bottle and make it a safer drink than the local water in many places in the world. (Wine acid is very refreshing, clean, and nonvolatile. It doesn't come off as acidic right away, like vinegar does. The family of wine acids, when taken together, give wine an acidity profile—or, in general terms, the way the wine hits you at first.)

Unlike other alcoholic beverages, wine is meant to be enjoyed with food. While someone might well enjoy sipping Chardonnay as a cocktail—or, for that matter, nursing a martini during dinner—the wine glass is happiest beside the tip of the dinner knife. Good food and good wine make each other taste even better, and there is a considerable body of rules and theories for properly matching food and wine. Fortunately, there is little or no penalty for deviating from these rules, because, in reality, most well-made wine is perfectly enjoyable with most foods.

Wine is good for you . . . maybe. Medical research suggests that moderate wine consumption might have healthful benefits. While several studies on the "French Paradox" conclude that specific antioxidants in red grape skins *may* contribute to longevity, perhaps it is the joyous occasions with family and friends at which wine is normally consumed—as much as the wine itself—that fortifies your life force and, thus, lengthens your stay on Earth. There are limits to such benefits, of course, and more wine is definitely not better for you.

Aside from everything else, wine is also an intoxicant, and a breathalyzer does not distinguish between a driver impaired by whisky and an inebriated wine connoisseur. Wine is among nature's most wonderful gifts to the human race, but it must be enjoyed in moderation. When consumed responsibly, wine is a source of profound happiness, yet, when drunk to excess, great wine is no less a destroyer of families and lives than cheap beer or rotgut whisky.

Great music can be transcribed or recorded, historic moments can be captured on film, and chemical reactions can be symbolized for posterity in equations. Every bottle of wine, however, offers a unique sensual experience that can only be memorialized in writing; for instance, a legendary wine such as Château Margaux 1900, while presently a decrepit shell of its former excellence, lives on in full glory in the elegant prose of professional wine scribes who have tasted this marvelous wine in its prime. And so the ability to translate a wine's flavors and aromas accurately into meaningful words is of paramount importance in the wine business. Reading about wines—while sipping some, ideally—will not only give you a wine education, it will also make you more familiar with the world around you in many ways. Knowledge of wine also entails some familiarity with history, law, politics, economics, geology, geography, biology, chemistry, and religion, as all of these disciplines have had some influence on the wine we drink, as you will soon see when you read on in this book.

Part 1

Wine 101

Chapter 1

A Brief History of Wine

ACCORDING TO THE United States Internal Revenue Service, wine is considered a manufactured product rather than agricultural produce. However, wine as we know it today is a natural extension of the vine and the soil, much less a manufactured product than other alcoholic drinks such as cinnamon schnapps or malt liquor. The adult beverage industry regularly test markets new and contrived products with flashy labels and chemically tweaked flavor profiles. One year it might be "dry beer," the next year "spiked lemonade," and a single success can more than pay for dozens of flops.

Wine, however, is different. Wine as we know it was not suddenly invented in the way that these other novelty drinks were. As noted in this book's Introduction, wine is an almost naturally occurring product, one that has evolved over many centuries. That being said, winemaking has benefited from advances in technology over the years. Lengthy histories of wine and winemaking have little relevance to most wine drinkers, so let us look at just the highlights of the past seventy or so centuries—the events and developments in wine and winemaking that have had the most significant influences on the wine we drink today. This sort of historical framework will help you to better understand and enjoy wine.

The Origins of Wine

Winemaking got its start, in all likelihood, somewhere in the Middle East, perhaps 7,000 years ago. The Fertile Crescent—the "cradle of civilization"—extends from Egypt to present-day Iraq. It was in these rich river valleys that early humans stopped roaming long enough to cultivate crops, and the grape was a sugar-rich staple of their diet. Undoubtedly, grape fermentation first occurred accidentally at some point, when someone let the grapes lay around for too long, and the fruit split open. The wild yeast that grew on the grape skin performed its magic, and someone probably ate these grapes and became intoxicated. This probably happened a few times before anyone got the picture. With no understanding of fermentation or the nature of alcohol, it is no wonder that the ancients ascribed supernatural qualities to wine and included it in religious rituals, a tradition that still lives on today.

While wine production probably got its start in the "cradle of civilization," it is important to note that this was the cradle of *Western* civilization; although other cultures were simultaneously developing in other parts of the world, traditions of viticulture (wine grape cultivation) never developed in the Far East or in the pre-Columbian Americas. Wild grapes indeed grow all over the world, but the Fertile Crescent had the right grapes for wine production: *Vitis vinifera*, the species native to the Caucasus mountain region to the north, which was probably brought south by seed to the fertile valleys.

As Western civilization spread forth from the Middle East, so too did wine spread, first throughout the Mediterranean, and then through continental Europe. This is why wine today may be thought of as "Eurocentric." While other cultures around the world have produced wine of some sort through the ages, fine wine became almost the exclusive dominion of Europe until the twentieth century, and virtually all of the newly developed wine regions in the world produce wine that harkens back to its European origins.

The Proliferation of Wine in the Ancient World

Grapes, and by extension the process of winemaking, spread to other areas as the ancient Mediterranean seafarers—first the Phoenicians and then the Greeks—brought the grapevine along in their travels and conquests. Beginning in 1400 B.C., they were responsible for the proliferation of vineyards throughout the Mediterranean basin. While the Greeks believed that the realm of the wine grape extended only as far north as did that of the fig and the olive, the Romans introduced viticulture steadily northward to its climatic limits in what is now Northern France and Germany during the first century A.D. We now know today that the finest wines are produced not in hot climates where the wine grape ripens without effort, but rather in cooler climates in which the grapes must struggle somewhat, where complete ripeness is achieved only after the full array of flavor components have had sufficient "hang" time to develop.

The Roman Influence

Well-aged wine was especially prized in ancient Rome. For the Romans to age some of their wines for twenty-five years, as some

Roman writings suggest, they must have either perfected the airtight seal for their storage vessels or enjoyed the taste of oxidized wine. Although the Egyptians first developed glassware in 1500 B.C., the Romans developed the technique of glass blowing, and they produced rather intricate wine glasses and serving vessels. However, Roman glass was not strong enough for wine bottles, and so they used ceramic amphorae for storing wine.

Other European Contributions

As the Romans were busy making their contributions, the wine-loving Celts of North-Central Europe were known to be using wooden barrels at the time of Julius Caesar's military campaign in Gaul around 50 B.C. The basic design of the wine barrel has changed little since ancient times: A bulge in the middle makes for easier rolling and handling; the dried staves swell slightly with wine to make a secure, air-tight seal; and the grain of the oak allows the wine to "breathe" slightly through its pores as it matures. This oaky presence is perhaps the most important legacy passed on from these early barrels. Oak adds a distinct flavor element to wine, a component that blends so naturally with wine's other flavors that wine consumers have come to expect a degree of oakiness in even the least expensive wines on the market.

Following the collapse of the Roman Empire in A.D. 476, Christian monasteries played an enormous role in the development of European wine. Their trial and error with different grape varieties in different soils, along with their meticulous record-keeping, is largely responsible for the development of winemaking traditions in Europe, particularly in France and Germany, which are now codified in law. This is why when you purchase a bottle of, say, Beaujolais, you know that it is made from 100 percent Gamay grapes. Centuries of experience has demonstrated that the Gamay grape is uniquely suited to the granite-rich soils in the Beaujolais region, and so no other red grape is permitted to be grown there. Strict regulation of grape varieties and other aspects of viticulture are common for quality wine in much of Europe, and this regulation is the cornerstone of most labeling law.

Winemaking Spreads to the New World

By the 1600s, European wine had become a highly refined product. The right grapes were planted in the right regions, and winemaking technique, though unscientific, benefited nonetheless from the previous millennium of trial and error. Meanwhile, the glass bottle, which had already been in existence for several centuries, and the cork stopper, known to the Greeks, finally got together in the seventeenth century. At this point, the combined technology of these two things made long-term wine storage possible. Soon thereafter it was discovered that certain red wines, such as Hermitage and Bordeaux, improved with patient cellaring in corked bottles.

Like the Phoenicians, Greeks, and Romans before them, European explorers to the new world brought their wine—and grapevines—along on their journeys. Although they found a new continent nearly covered with wild grapevines, the New-World fruit was a barely recognizable, distant cousin of *Vitis vinifera*. And so the Spanish, English, and French settlers attempted to grow the European vines in American soil. They found little success in the Eastern United States, where the harsh winters and native vine pests sabotaged their efforts. However, as the Spanish *conquistadors* ventured into what is now California, their imported "Mission" vines found a happy home in the loose, volcanic soils and the endless sunshine, and so Spanish missions in Southern California produced European-style wine, sacramental or otherwise, with ease.

Having failed to propagate European *vinifera* varieties, wine-makers in the Northeast built a gigantic wine industry in the early 1800s based on native grape varieties (*Vitis labrusca*) and their cross-ings—Concord, Catawba, and Delaware were three of the most commonly planted varieties. By midcentury, New York and Ohio stood tall as the leading wine producing states in the new nation. Then somebody found a gold nugget in a river in California.

Beginning in 1848, the Californian gold rush brought half a million people to what became known as the Golden State. The gold rush ended by 1862, but the new residents found in North-Central California an agricultural "Eden" in which many different crops—including European grape varieties—could ripen to perfection. The mediocre Mission grape was eventually replaced by superior grape varieties transplanted from the finest wine regions in Europe, and it was soon obvious that it was easier to cultivate high-quality, European wine grapes in California than anywhere else in the world.

Meanwhile, Northeasterners were trying to figure out why these fancy imported vines couldn't survive. The *phylloxera* vine louse attacks vine roots, eventually killing the grapevine. Because these pests are indigenous to the Northeastern United States, over time, native *labrusca* vines developed resistance to *phylloxera*. European vines, however, had no reason to develop such resistance and, there-fore, easily succumbed to this deadly vine louse after a season or two. To make matters worse, native American vines were foolishly imported to Europe, complete with the *phylloxera* louse on their roots. The louse soon spread, and the defenseless vineyards of Europe were quickly destroyed wholesale; all but the most remote fell prey.

Because the worldwide wine industry had, by the middle 1800s, become so economically important, it is no wonder that the *phylloxera* scourge was so lavishly attacked and an answer so quickly found. The relatively simple solution was to graft *vinifera* vines onto *labrusca* rootstock, and this technique is practiced to this day. Amid the resulting widespread economic carnage, *phylloxera* had a curious (if comparatively minor) benefit—it caused talented winemakers to seek healthy vineyards elsewhere in order to ply their trade. The wine of the Rioja region in Spain, for instance, owes much to the influx of French winemakers who fled *phylloxera*-ravaged Bordeaux in the 1860s.

Setbacks in the Prohibition Era

It was perhaps to be expected that *phylloxera* would eventually come full circle and spread to the vineyards of California. However, while Californian vintners were winning their initial round against *phylloxera* (the louse would reappear in the 1990s), a destructive force more powerful than any vine pest was poised to destroy most of what the Golden State's pioneering *vignerons* had created in the preceding half-century.

As the American wine industry was beginning to flourish and gain worldwide recognition for its quality in the mid-1800s, the seeds of its near-destruction, in the form of anti-alcohol sentiment, were also taking root. Spurred on by religious fervor as well as justifiable antipathy toward the proliferation of saloons, the "dry" movement gained power one church, one county, and one state at a time until anti-alcohol crusaders prevailed as a majority. Nearly a century after the movement began, the infamous Volstead Act (the law enacted to implement the 18th Amendment, or "Prohibition") outlawed "the manufacture, sale, or transportation of intoxicating liquors," effective

January 16, 1920. The destruction of the American wine industry by the misguided zealots who supported the 18th Amendment was severe. Uprooted vineyards and abandoned equipment were common sights. However, many Californian growers and producers found creative ways to remain in the business.

Ingenuity Ensues

Medicinal wine and wine-based tonics were not outlawed. When chilled, the medicinal additives settled to the bottom, leaving a somewhat palatable wine. Cooking wine could still be produced, so long as it was salted (so as to be undrinkable). Sacramental and religious wines were still sold, especially to newly minted "rabbis" whose "synagogues" were really private drinking clubs. Most significant of all was a loophole in the Prohibition law that allowed the home production of "fruit juice"—up to 200 gallons per year! Since it is easier to make wine than beer or whiskey, the demand for grapes soared until 1925, when a huge surplus knocked the bottom out of the grape market.

Reworking Wine Post-Prohibition

Prohibition was repealed by the 21st Amendment, which, once formally proposed, was quickly ratified by the states on December 5, 1933. And so, after nearly fourteen disastrous years that saw the loss of hundreds of millions of dollars in federal tax revenue, the nearly total destruction of America's promising young wine industry, and the vacuum-filling rise of organized crime in the United States, alcohol was suddenly legal again. As the industry rebuilt itself after the repeal of Prohibition, it found a market much changed in its thirteen-year hiatus. The quality of wine was very poor, in part because California grape growers were raising grapes that shipped well, rather than grapes that made fine wine. The public preferred "dessert wines"—fortified wines, actually—to dry table wines. Nonetheless, the American wine industry slowly recovered.

Wine production became increasingly scientific and standardized during the twentieth century. In an effort to establish consistent standards for all of the important aspects of wine production—including region of origin, grape varieties, minimum alcohol content, and maximum vineyard yields—France enacted a series of laws beginning in 1905 collectively known as the Appellation d'Origine Contrôlée (AOC) laws. These laws guard the famous place-names of France and guarantee that wines bearing their names have met rigorous government standards. In 1963 Italy followed suit with her own set of laws: Denominazione di Origine Controllata (DOC) and Denominazione di Origine Controllata e Garantita (DOCG). With these laws, Europe set the standard for the entire wine world in legislating the integrity of wine. Beginning in 1983, the United States government followed suit, enacting a series of laws recognizing carefully delineated "American Viticultural Areas" (AVAs) for the distinctive characteristics of their wines. (See Chapter 9, Wine Regions, for more on these wine laws.)

The Wine Boom in America

The American wine boom really began with the affluence of the late 1950s. Wine was attractive to educated suburbanites, especially those wealthy enough to travel abroad. Wine, which to most of the wine-drinking world is a simple beverage, had become a status symbol in the United States. A few role models helped. When John F. Kennedy was sworn in he brought with him, among other things, a new sense of internationalism and his wife Jackie, who loved all things French. As a result, French restaurants—and French wines—became very trendy.

In 1962, the film version of Ian Fleming's book, *Dr. No*, was released. The protagonist, British agent 007, had expensive tastes in cars, women, and wine. From a kitchen in a Boston television studio, Julia Child taught a generation of Americans how to prepare French cuisine—and to match it with wine. By 1970, Americans were drinking well over a gallon of wine per person per year.

New products appeared in wine stores to meet the growing demand. Portuguese rosé, which perhaps blazed the trail for American White Zinfandel, hit the shelves around this time. Lancer's and Mateus, the two most common, were slightly fizzy, fruity, and sweet. The fact that they were imported from Europe gave these quaint wines sufficient cachet in the market. From West Germany came Liebfraumilch, a flowery, fruity, and slightly sweet blend of Riesling and other lesser grape varieties. Americans were switching back from the sweet, fortified ports and sherries to table wines, but they hadn't entirely lost their sweet tooth.

American Wine Hits Its Stride

Meanwhile, California's reputation for world-class fine wines rapidly grew. In the early 1970s resourceful winemakers, many educated in their craft at the University of California at Davis, developed a whole new genre of California wine—high-alcohol, big, fruity wine that took full advantage of the long California growing season. In a now-infamous side-by-side blind tasting against fine French wines held in 1976 (with French judges!), the American wines defeated the finest wines of France and put the wine universe on notice that California could produce world-class wines. American winemakers swelled with pride.

The market for varietal Cabernet Sauvignons was hot in that decade, whereas the market for varietal Zinfandel was not. Unfortunately, many growers had acre upon acre of Zinfandel vines whose grapes matured effortlessly in the California sunshine and provided blenders with a dependable workhorse of a grape. This surplus was the inspiration for "White Zinfandel." This fruity, pink, and slightly sweet rosé, a little classier than its Portuguese predecessor, found its way into every corner of the market. For many customers, White Zinfandel was their first taste of wine. The popularity of White Zinfandel helped drive wine consumption in the United States up to two gallons per person per year.

The wine industry found it necessary to develop White Zinfandel because Americans in the 1970s showed a strong preference for white wine over red. While premium Cabernet Sauvignon was in demand and selling well, California growers found the Pinot Noir grape troublesome, and bothered little with Merlot which, they believed, had no future.

That is, until the medical community pondered the so-called "French Paradox." Why do the French—who smoke more than Americans, eat more red meat, and exercise less—have fewer heart attacks? Upon asking this question, medical researchers came back with a surprising answer. It is because the French drink red wine! Due to these findings, health-conscious Americans changed from white wine to red in the blink of an eye. And it was Merlot they turned to *en masse*.

Red Wine Catches On in the United States

The Merlot grape has a well-deserved reputation for making soft, fruity wine—the perfect red wine for white-wine drinkers who never got used to the tannic edge of most Cabernet Sauvignons. Merlot has been used for centuries in Bordeaux to soften Cabernet-based wine, yet it was considered too insubstantial to make wine by itself outside of the Pomerol district of Bordeaux. The rapidity with which Americans turned to Merlot is a measure of how highly they prize a "quick fix" to a medical quandary. "Drink red wine, live longer!" Simple. Except there wasn't nearly enough Merlot to go around. The price of Merlot grapes shot skyward, prompting growers to plant in less-than-ideal growing areas, increase their crop yields, and harvest grapes from younger vines. All of this had an unfortunate result—inexpensive Merlot can often be a harsh, angular wine instead of the soft, lush wine typically associated with the Merlot grape. But the wine-buying public hasn't seemed to mind, and the Merlot boom is the legacy of the "French Paradox."

There is good news for Merlot fans, however: All those recently planted Merlot vines are maturing, and this should result in better Merlot at stable prices. In the meantime, it is likely that the red-wine converts of the Merlot boom, looking for quality and value, will develop a taste for the other important red varietals: Cabernet Sauvignon, Zinfandel, Pinot Noir, and especially Syrah. This noble variety from France's Rhône Valley—known as "Shiraz" in Australia—has demonstrated an ability to produce world-class wine in many different parts of the world in the past decade.

Chapter 2

Types of Wine

WINE LABELS USUALLY—but not always—tell us what we need to know about the wine we are buying. Certain terms are obvious and self-explanatory, while others may seem obscure or misleading. Here is an explanation of some label terms you are likely to see.

Table Wine (Where Else Would You Put a Wineglass?)

The term "table wine" has several different meanings. On European labels it may suggest common, everyday wine of little distinction, not good enough for any of the "quality wine" designations. In some regions—particularly in Tuscany—it might indicate that a wine, though perfectly good, does not conform to traditional, local wine-making practices and, thus, is ineligible to display the name of its birthplace. As used on wine labels in the United States, "table wine" is by federal law grape wine, either sweet or dry, and not in excess of 14 percent alcohol. Some Californian producers use the term "table wine" when they don't use enough of any one grape variety (75 percent) for "varietal" labeling. For our purposes in this book we consider "table wine" to be still (not sparkling) wine with alcohol below 16 percent and dry (with no perceptible sugar) or only slightly sweet—in other words, wine that you would typically have with dinner. This would include dry white wine, dry red wine, dry rosé wine, and slightly sweet rosé wine.

White Table Wine

White table wine isn't really white. White table wine is made from green-, yellow-, or even dark-skinned grapes that are pressed in such a way that the light-colored juice runs freely from the grapes without drawing much color or extract from the skins. The naturally occurring sugar in the juice then ferments to between 8 percent and 15 percent alcohol, leaving almost no residual sugar behind. "Chardonnay" is a white table wine, one that is labeled by the primary grape variety used in its production. "Sancerre" is another white table wine, labeled by its geographic origin. To be labeled as "Sancerre" the wine must conform to French government standards dictating the grape variety (Sauvignon Blanc in this case), crop yield per acre, and other factors.

(For lists of specific white table wine recommendations, see Chapter 8, Varietal Wines, Grape by Grape.)

Red Table Wine

Red table wine ranges in hue from light brick red to deep purple to almost black. The color comes from the skins. Unlike white grapes, the grapes for red wine production are crushed, and the juice and the skins get a prolonged soaking (up to a month) before the mash of crushed grapes (the "must") is gently pressed to separate the juice. While some red grapes, especially those grown in the hotter parts of California, may develop very high sugar levels, red wine, like white wine, rarely ferments to levels higher than 15 percent on its own. Like white table wines, red table wines may be labeled by grape variety, geographic origin, or by a brand name.

(For lists of specific red table wine recommendations, see Chapter 8, Varietal Wines, Grape by Grape.)

Rosé Wine

There are great white wines and there are great red wines. However, we never hear anyone call a rosé wine great. Perhaps that is because rosé wine has characteristics of both red and white wine, but not the best characteristics; kind of like cross-breeding a supermodel and a physicist, only to produce offspring with the scientist's looks and the model's brains.

Rosé table wine can be made several different ways: Red wine grapes (such as Zinfandel) may be vinified as if they were white wine grapes, with just enough skin contact to impart a "blush" of pinkness; or, more simply, unfinished red and white wine may be blended in such proportions as to yield a light, pink-colored wine. Rosé table wines are often bottled with a hint or more of sweetness, perhaps because they might otherwise be charmless. However, the bone-dry rosé table wines of France and Spain are considered to be the best in the world, if only enjoyable during the hot summer months, when food and wine are less formal.

Rosés of the World

Name	Region	Price
Beringer White Zinfandel	California	$5
Château de Mongueret "Rosé de Loire"	Loire Valley, France	$9
Viña Sardosol	Navarra, Spain	$11
Bonny Doon, "Vin Gris de Cigare" Pink Wine	California	$12
Canto Perdix, Tavel	Rhône, France	$15
Château d'Aqueria, Tavel	Rhône, France	$15

Note: In all lists of recommended wines, prices and availability may vary.

Sparkling Wine, or Bubbly

"Come, for I am drinking stars!" So said Benedictine cellar master Dom Pérignon, according to legend, when he tasted the first "champagne." (In reality, the bubbles in champagne came long after the monk's death.)

A generation ago, a dutiful husband knew enough to pick up a bottle of champagne on his way home from work for special occasions such as his wife's birthday, their anniversary, St. Valentine's Day, and New Year's Eve. These may well have been the only four times that a couple drank wine of any sort. Today, however, the American public is far savvier when it comes to choosing wine, and the wine dollars that once went toward champagne might now be spent on very good Chardonnay or Merlot. Wine is a regular part of many people's lifestyles these days.

However, champagne has become a victim of the wine boom, in large part because it has never lost its association with celebrations and special events. That is a pity. Quality champagnes and other sparkling wines are simply good wines with bubbles, and they are generally excellent food wines. Despite the common perception, they need not be any more expensive than anything else you would drink.

The Origins of Champagne

Champagne derives its name from the district in Northern France where it is produced—a region in which wine has been made since Roman times. It was not until the early 1800s that "champagne" became synonymous with effervescent white (or pink) wine.

The bubbles in champagne are the result of a second fermentation that takes place within the sealed bottle. When yeast cells transform sugar into ethyl alcohol, they produce carbon dioxide gas as well. Over several centuries, champagne producers perfected the technique of putting still (nonsparkling) wine in sturdy bottles, adding yeast and sugar, and sealing the bottle with a temporary stopper to keep the carbon dioxide from escaping. In order to produce a crystal-clear sparkling wine, the remaining dead yeast cells must be quickly removed so as not to lose the effervescence. This technique is known as the "Champagne method" and often appears on wine labels as *"méthode champenoise."*

Grape Varieties in Sparkling Wines

French champagne is made from three different grape varieties: the dark-skinned Pinot Noir and Pinot Meunier, which barely ripen so far north; and Chardonnay. Bottles labeled "Blanc de Noirs" are made solely from the Pinots, while "Blanc de Blancs" is made entirely from Chardonnay. Sparkling wine producers around the world tend to use

Pinot Noir and/or Chardonnay, while Pinot Meunier is rarely culti-vated outside of the Champagne district.

Other Types of Sparkling Wines

The French prefer to keep the name "champagne" for wines pro-duced in their Champagne district by this painstaking method. How-ever, sparkling wine is produced throughout the world, under a variety of names, including:

- **Cava** from Spain
- **Sekt** from Germany
- **Prosecco** from the Veneto region of Italy
- **Sparkling Shiraz**, a highly unusual but delicious version produced in Australia

Much to the annoyance of the French, it is allowable under United States law to label sparkling wine as "champagne" (with a small "c") as long as the label indicates the geographic origin (such as "California" or "New York State") and the method by which the wine got its sparkle. Aside from the labor-intensive (and expensive) *méthode champenoise*, there are other, less expensive ways to produce bubbles, such as the "charmat bulk process" or the "transfer method." These terms—or their euphemisms—will appear on the wine label.

Champagne and sparkling wine labels will often (but not always) give an indication of the beverage's degree of sweetness. In the Champagne method, sugar is often added to the bottle after the dead yeast is removed in order to balance the flavor. Following is a quick listing of common label terms that indicate champagne's level of sweetness:

- **Brut** indicates an added sugar content of 15 grams per liter (about a tablespoon per bottle) or less.
- **Extra Dry** is slightly sweeter.
- **Demi-sec** is sweet enough for dessert.
- **Brut Nature or Brut Sauvage** indicates that no sugar has been added.

Champagne and Sparkling Wine from Around the World

Name	Region	Price
Zardetto Prosecco NV	Veneto, Italy	$10
Segura Viudas "Aria Brut" Cava	Catalonia, Spain	$10
Gruet Blanc de Noirs NV	New Mexico	$13
Veuve Clicquot NV "Yellow Label"	Champagne, France	$35
Roederer Estate "Brut L'Hermitage"	Anderson Valley, CA	$36
Bollinger "Special Cuvée" Brut	Champagne, France	$50
Schramsberg Reserve Cuvée	California	$60
Laurent-Perrier "Cuvée Rosé Brut" NV	Champagne, France	$75
Moët et Chandon, Cuvée Dom Pérignon	Champagne, France	$110
Krug "Grande Cuvée" NV	Champagne, France	$140

Dessert Wine

Dessert wine, in its finest forms, displays all of the charms one expects of a great wine—intriguing aromas, layers of complex flavors, velvety texture, and a long, memorable finish. On top of all that, dessert wine is sweet enough to satisfy your inner trick-or-treater. Dessert wine truly embodies the best of everything wine has to offer in one glass. A great dessert wine has enough complexity to seduce the most jaded veteran wine lover's palate, yet it also captivates the neophyte with its luscious sweetness. While sweetness is the common denominator, there are enough different types and styles of dessert wine to constitute a parallel wine universe.

What Makes Wine Sweet?

Sweet wine is certainly not a recent development. Prior to the advent of tightly sealed bottles, wine made from raisined grapes was prized by the ancients for its sweetness as well as for its longevity, and it is likely that the earliest wines were often sweet as a result of incomplete fermentations. Modern dessert wines, sweet by design, are characterized by very high sugar levels perfectly balanced with piercing acidity. These wines come by their sweetness via several different paths, nearly always beginning with naturally occurring glucose and fructose. Concentrations of these grape sugars increase in proportion to ripeness, and fully ripe grapes usually have a sugar content sufficient to ferment into 12 percent alcohol by volume. The unfermented (residual) sugar in sweet dessert wines is the result of one of several factors—raisining, extreme ripeness, a freeze late in the harvest, fermentation-stopping fortification with brandy . . . or an infection of the mold *botrytis cinerea*, also known as "noble rot."

Just as the first wine in history was most likely the result of grapes inadvertently allowed to ferment, the first dessert wine as we know it was probably the result of a happy accident of nature. Just imagine an exasperated *vigneron* discovering a few rows of grotesquely moldy grapes and then bravely vinifying them, only to find that he has produced a delicious, sweet nectar.

Great European Dessert Wines

The vineyards of the Sauternes district in the Bordeaux region are particularly susceptible to the *botrytis* mold, which draws water from the grape while leaving the sugars alone. Because much of the water has been stolen from the affected grapes, it takes many times more grapes to yield a given quantity of wine, which commands a correspondingly steep price. The great Château d'Yquem of Sauternes is generally regarded as the world's standard-bearing dessert wine and fetches about $140 per half bottle upon release.

There are many excellent Sauternes available for a fraction of d'Yquem's price, and *botrytis*-influenced dessert wines are produced elsewhere in France and in other countries. Lesser-known *botrytized* French dessert wines include Quarts-de-Chaume from the Loire Valley and Sélection des Grains Nobles (SGN) wines from Alsace. Meanwhile, on the other side of the Vosges Mountains from Alsace, German jawbreakers such as "Beerenauslese" and "Trockenbeerenauslese" appear on wine labels to indicate the influence of the noble rot in Germany's sweetest Rieslings and other wines.

Frozen Grapes

In addition to the wines mentioned above, Germany is perhaps best known as the original source of "eiswein," dessert wine made from grapes that have frozen on the vine. Frozen grapes leave much of their water behind as ice crystals, and thus yield wine with an unctuous and heavenly concentration of fruity sweetness. Unlike Sauternes, which can often display a deliciously muddled array of rich flavors, eiswein's flavors are typically as clear as a January night sky. It's almost as if the requisite freezing of the grapes—to 18°F for an extended period—somehow purifies the soul of the wine.

Buying and Storing Dessert Wine

The vast majority of dessert wines are offered in half-bottles (375ml), which is the best way to buy them. A little sweetness goes a long way: A half-bottle provides enough dessert wine for four or even six people. Sugar can act as a natural wine preservative, so an unfinished bottle of dessert wine will keep in the fridge a little longer than will a partially empty bottle of dry wine. The high alcohol content of the stronger fortified wines allows them to keep for many weeks after opening. ❧

It is only natural, then, that innovative winemakers would find a less labor-intensive alternative to handpicking frozen grapes under a bone-chilling Arctic cold front. Winemaker Randall Grahm of Bonny Doon Vineyard in California was the first to short-circuit the natural grape freeze process successfully, simply by putting Muscat grapes in the freezer for a spell and then vinifying the frozen results. Instead of co-opting the term "eiswein" (or even "ice wine"), he playfully named the sweet results "Muscat Vin de Glaciere," that is, "Wine of the Icebox." Other wineries have been quicker to borrow the increasingly marketable "eiswein" or "ice wine" terms for wines produced by artificial freezing. However, the U.S. government recently formalized its long-standing objection to such terminology for American wines. Consequently, the terminology's use on wine labels is now prohibited unless the grapes actually freeze while still on the vine. The United States is not the only other country to venture into "ice wine" territory. The Canadian wine industry benefits from reliably frigid weather in late autumn and has become world famous for its consistent production of excellent—and genuine—ice wine.

Other Sweet Wines from Around the World

Never to be outdone by the French, Germans, or anyone else, Italian winemakers, from the Alps down to Sicily, offer their own assortment of sweet wines. There are sweet versions of Amarone, a heavy red made from dried grapes, and late-harvest versions of Soave, both from the Veneto region. Tuscany offers Vin Santo, an amber-colored wine made from dried grapes. And from Piedmont come low-alcohol sweet sparklers, both red (Brachetto d'Acqui) and white (Moscato d'Asti).

Elsewhere in the world, Tokaji Aszu, "the poor man's d'Yquem," is one of the world's great dessert wines and has been produced in Hungary since the 1600s by blending a base wine with *aszu* paste, a mash of *botrytis*-affected grapes, in varying proportions. Less famous dessert wines of one type or another are presently produced in nearly every wine-producing region in the world, but only one is sweetened by the actual addition of sugar.

Dessert Champagne

The art of champagne making, the *méthode champenoise*, has been slowly perfected over the last three centuries. After completion of the second fermentation and a lengthy repose on the dead yeast cells, the champagne bottle is "disgorged," that is, the temporary stopper is removed from the bottle and the dead yeast is quickly removed. At this crucial stage of production the sweetness of the final bottling is determined by the *dosage*, the addition of a mixture of wine and sugar syrup. Champagne labeled as "brut" has less than 15 grams per liter of added sugar and tastes quite dry, while dessert champagne labeled as "demi-sec" has between 33 and 50 grams per liter and is noticeably sweet.

These dessert champagnes constitute only a tiny fraction of overall champagne production. Dessert wine production among *méthode champenoise* producers outside of the Champagne district is even rarer, the most notable example being Schramsberg Cremant Demi-Sec, an ambrosially sweet sparkler made from the Flor grape, a cross of Gewürztraminer and Semillon, in Napa Valley.

Dessert Wine from Ten Different Countries

Name	Region	Price
Sarocco, Moscato d'Asti	Piedmont, Italy	$16
Gran Barquero Pedro Ximenez (750ml)	Montilla-Moriles, Spain	$16
Campbell's Muscat (375ml)	Rutherglen, Australia	$17
Hermann J. Wiemer "Select" Ice Wine (375ml)	Finger Lakes, NY	$35
Kracher, Cuvée Beerenauslese (375ml)	Niederösterreich, Austria	$35
Klein Contantia, "Vin de Constance" (500ml)	South Africa	$35
Inniskillin, Vidal Ice Wine (375ml)	Niagra, Canada	$50
Château Raymond-Lafon Sauternes (375ml)	Bordeaux, France	$50
Royal Tokaji Wine Company, Essencia 1995 (500ml)	Hungary	$140
Keller Trockenbeerenauslese (375ml)	Rheinhessen, Germany	$200

Fortified Wine

Fortified wines came into being following the discovery and refinement of the distillation process, the partial vaporization of a fermented liquid in order to separate and thus concentrate its alcohol. When produced from wine, the result is known as brandy, and it was discovered that, when added to a fermenting vat in sufficient concentration (to about 18 to 20 percent alcohol), brandy stops the yeasts in their tracks, resulting in a wine with noticeable sweetness from the residual, unfermented sugar that is stronger in alcohol than typical table wine. (Hence the term "fortified.")

These fortified wines, it was found, are relatively immune to the normally damaging jostle and heat on the high seas, and thus they shipped easily and found favor in far away England. The best-known of the fortified wines are:

- **Port** (from Portugal)
- **Sherry** (from Spain)
- **Marsala** (from Sicily)
- **Madeira** (from the island of the same name)

The French, meanwhile, have some lesser-known fortified wines of their own—vin doux naturel, or "naturally sweet wine." The best known of these—the orange-hued Muscat Beaumes-de-Venise and the deep red, Grenache-based Banyuls—are both fortified with spirits to about 15 percent alcohol.

Not all fortified wine is sweet, however. Fortified wines are recognized just as much for their role in cooking recipes as they are for their drinkability. In general, the dry versions of fortified wine are superior for cooking, and are often served as apéritifs, while the sweet versions are key members of the family of dessert wines. (For more on cooking with wine, see Chapter 13, Wine and Food.)

Port

Port, or Porto, comes from Portugal. The name, however, comes not from the country but from the city of Oporto, at the mouth of the Douro River. As the only red fortified wine, it has natural appeal among red-wine lovers who prize Port's capacity to improve with age in the bottle for many decades.

Port is sold in several different styles—Vintage, Tawny, and Ruby are the principal versions. Vintage Port, the most expensive of these, is also the easiest to produce—as long as nature cooperates; Tawny Port, so named for its brownish cast, is the result of long barrel-aging; and Ruby Port, named for its bright, unoxidized color, is an inexpensive style that is perfect for neophytes and fine cooking.

Port is made from several different red varieties that grow to extreme ripeness in Portugal's hot Douro Valley. The fruity Souzão grape, the dark-colored "Tintas"—Tinta Cao and Tinta Francisca— and the Cabernet Franc-like Touriga are blended along with other varieties in various proportions. A white Port is also produced, although it is not nearly as prized as the red versions. All (red) Port, then, starts out as "musts" from these varieties, which are allowed to ferment half way to dryness before the addition of brandy. Since half of the natural sugar remains unfermented, the resulting fortified wine is sweet. It then begins its life in "Port pipes" (138-gallon storage casks).

Vintage Port

After two years in storage a vintage may be "declared" by agreement of a majority of the Port producers. This means that the Port from that particular vintage is deemed to be of sufficient quality to justify offering it as top-of-the-line Vintage Port. Vintage Port is then bottled and is best aged for at least a decade. Because Vintage Port ages in the bottle, often for several decades, it deposits a substantial amount of sediment in the bottle.

Vintage Port has always been quite popular among the British, and when paired with a wedge of Stilton, the deluxe cheese of England, you have a match made in heaven. The pungent saltiness of the cheese complements the sweet richness of Vintage Port beautifully.

Tawny Port

Unlike Vintage Port, which is transferred to bottles in its youth, Tawny Port may remain in the cask for ten, twenty, or even thirty years. "Tawny" refers to the pale brown hue of these fortified wines after so long in the cask, where oxidation occurs more readily than in the bottle. With the high alcohol guarding against the formation of vinegar, the oxidation in this case improves the flavor over time. The fruit flavors of youth evolve into mellower, more subtle flavors, and the Port becomes seemingly less sweet.

Tawny Port requires far more blending skills than does vintage Port. Unless labeled "Port of the Vintage" (another form of Tawny Port), most Tawnies are blends of ports from several different years chosen for their complementary characteristics.

Ruby Port

Ruby Port, named for its bright crimson color, is a blend of young, lesser lots of Port. Again, the blender's art is of importance. Lesser lots (casks) of Port may be skillfully blended to produce an inexpensive and delicious Ruby Port.

The forthright flavors of the Ruby variety make it a perfect choice for recipes that call for this Port. The flavors of Ruby Port will endure the cooking process far better than will the other types. Also, Ruby Port is a perfect introduction to Port as you begin to explore fortified wines.

Recommended Port Producers

Croft	Graham
Dow	Cockburn
Fonseca	Warre
Taylor Fladgate	

Sherry

Like the other types of fortified wine, Sherry owes its popularity to the British. In fact, the name "Sherry" is an Anglicization of "Jerez," the port city on the coast of Spain from which Sherry is shipped.

Sherry is made by fortifying dry white wine made from the Palomino grape grown in Southern Spain. Among wine lovers, Sherry is not as well respected as Port, perhaps because Sherry is generally less "wine-like" and complex than Port. As a result, quality Sherry is often overlooked and underpriced. And yet, quality Sherry can be an ideal substitute for a variety of hard liquor drinks.

Whereas Port, particularly vintage Port, is perceived as closely akin to fine wine by consumers, quality Sherry is regarded as a manufactured product by many people, more like liquor than wine. Indeed, the aging, fortification, and blending processes for Sherry are far more involved than those for Vintage Port.

How Sherry Is Made

All Sherry begins its life in the warm, dry vineyards of Southern Spain. Here the Palomino grape, a variety of little use aside from Sherry production, is made into dry, still wine. This wine, called mosto, is initially fortified with brandy to an alcohol level of 15 percent and permitted to age in the presence of air. While contact with air would destroy most wines at this stage, the partially fortified mosto thrives on it. In most (but not all) of these huge barrels, a cushion of spongy yeast, called flor, develops on the surface of the wine.

In barrels with ample flor development, the wine beneath the layer of yeast is protected from oxidation and remains pale in color. The flor yeast also imparts flavor on the wine and further concentrates the alcoholic content. Sherry from these barrels is generally called "fino" and may become one of the three paler types of Sherry—Fino itself, Manzanilla, or Amontillado.

The barrels that develop little or no flor yeast yield "oloroso" Sherry, which is finished as one of the darker styles—dry Oloroso itself, sweet Amoroso, or very sweet cream Sherry. An especially rare type of Sherry is Palo Cortado, an Oloroso that develops flor yeast late in its life and can combine the finest qualities of both Finos and Olorosos.

Because the alcohol in Fino Sherries is concentrated by the flor yeast, these types of Sherries are given additional fortification only as required by importers worldwide. In Spain, Fino Sherry is often not additionally fortified and can be found at 16 percent alcohol. As such, this type of Sherry will not survive indefinitely in an opened bottle.

In contrast, the darker Oloroso Sherries usually receive a second fortification that raises the alcoholic strength to 18 to 20 percent. Because of this, Olorosos can live for a long time in the bottle after it is opened.

The blending process used in Sherry production, called the "solera" process, is unique. Barrels of young Sherry are connected to older barrels in such a manner that Sherries from different years are blended; this is why there are no vintage Sherries. You may, however, find an expensive Sherry with a year on the label. This is usually the vintage year of the oldest Sherry in the solera blend, and it might even be more than 100 years old.

Types of Sherries

There are several different types of Sherries, which range in color from light to dark, and in flavor from dry to sweet. These include:

- **Fino:** This is both the general name of the unfinished flor Sherries and the name of one of the finished products within that group. This Sherry is pale, dry, and best served chilled as an apéritif in the hot summer.
- **Manzanilla:** This is a pale, dry, fino Sherry that comes from the coastal town of Sanlúcar de Barrameda. Because it matures in casks stored near the sea, it acquires a tangy salty flavor from the coastal air. Serve it with tapas.
- **Amontillado:** This Sherry was made famous by Edgar Allan Poe's short story "The Cask of Amontillado." It is most notable for its nut-like flavor and aroma. These characteristics, along with a light brown color, can develop when a fino-type Sherry ages. Like the other fino types, Amontillado is a before-dinner drink, though better served at room temperature. While the paler fino types are most enjoyable in the hot summer, Amontillado is something of an autumn apéritif with its darker, richer flavors.
- **Oloroso:** Like Fino Sherry, Oloroso Sherry is both the name of a category of Sherries—those unaffected by flor—and the name of one of the finished products in this category. There is a popular perception that darker Sherries are, by definition, sweeter. This is not so, however. Oloroso Sherry itself is, in its natural state,

quite dry. Good Oloroso is richly flavored, full-bodied, and medium-brown in color.

• **Amoroso:** Dry Oloroso Sherry is sometimes sweetened by the addition of sweet, concentrated wine made for this purpose from Moscatel or Pedro Ximenez grapes. The result is Amoroso Sherry, a sweet after-dinner drink. Similarly, Amoroso can be darkened with the addition of specially prepared "coloring wine." Brown sherry is an especially dark version of Amoroso sherry.

• **Cream:** The sweetest of Sherries, if not the darkest, is Cream Sherry, first developed in Bristol, England. The widespread success of Harvey's Bristol Cream notwithstanding, Cream Sherry (even Harvey's) can be an enjoyable after-dinner drink.

Recommended Sherry Producers
Domecq   Osborne
Emilio Lustau   Savory & James
Gonzalez Byass

Other Fortified Wines

Whereas Port and Sherry are generally enjoyed as beverages, Madeira and Marsala are more commonly used for cooking. If you find that you enjoy Sherry and Port, you might want to experiment with these.

Madeira

Madeira is a small Portuguese-governed island in the Atlantic Ocean off the northwest coast of Africa. The most common of the eponymous fortified wines that it produces are used for cooking, but the better ones are consumed as cocktails. The early American colonists used to drink Madeira, so the island has a long history of producing and exporting its goods. Madeira is heated during the production process. It was discovered that heat improved the taste of the wine in the 1600s when Madeira was shipped across the Atlantic in hot cargo ships.

Light brown in color, Madeira can be sweet or dry. The four primary types of Madeira are:

- **Sercial:** the driest and most acidic Madeira
- **Verdelho:** medium-dry
- **Bual:** rich and raisiny
- **Malmsey:** a British corruption of Malvasia, a grape variety; the sweetest Madeira

The best Madeira is often aged for many decades and is a rare treat. If you don't see one of these four names on the bottle, you are getting an inferior quality Madeira. Think you're ready to venture into the world of Madeira wines? Start exploring this variety by comparing a pale Sercial to a dark Malmsey to figure out which style you like best.

Recommended Madeira Producers
Cossart Gordon
Veiga-Franca
Blandy's
Colombo

Marsala

Named for the town on the western tip of Sicily, Marsala is a brown-colored fortified wine made from the green-skinned Catarralto grape, a local variety. After harvesting, the grapes are dried prior to fermentation, which raises the sugar level. After fortification, Marsala is often sweetened and darkened with grape juice syrup. Barrel-aging mellows its flavors. Of all the fortified wines, Marsala is the least distinctive as a beverage and is best kept in the kitchen. Marsala comes in two styles, dry and sweet.

Recommended Marsala Producers
Florio
Pelligrino
Lombardo
Rallo

Kosher Wine

To be kosher, wine must be made by strictly Sabbath-observing Jews, although they might well be advised by professional wine-makers who have never visited any house of worship. Additionally, kosher wine must not be produced from young vines, and, in Israel, the vineyards must lie fallow (unused) for one harvest every seven years. Wine can be labeled "kosher for Passover" to indicate that it has not come into contact with bread or leavened dough products, and those labeled *mevushal* kosher have been boiled, rendering it useless for pagan rituals while ensuring that it remains kosher after being touched or served by a non-Jew. This boiling sounds like a harsh process, but one particular *grand cru* Burgundy, Château Corton-Grancey, is famously pasteurized every vintage without any negative effect. (Legendary Kosher winemaker Baron Herzog cleverly obtained permission from a rabbinical council to bring his *mevushal* wines to the boiling point of alcohol, significantly lower than that of water.)

So kosher wine, like nonkosher wine, can come in any imaginable style and range, from inexpensive to world-class great. And yet, many of us share a preconceived notion of what kosher wine tastes like . . . grapey and sweet. It is important to remember that there is not a single mention in the Old Testament, not in any Book, of the Concord grape.

The Origins of American Kosher Wine

Jewish immigrants came to the United States from Europe in several waves during the early twentieth century, and New York City was their usual port of entry. With the Californian wine industry still toddling and imports still uncommon, it fell to the local wineries in and around New York to produce the kosher wine necessary for observing the Sabbath and holidays. The native Concord grape of the species *Vitis labrusca* thrived in the nearby vineyards where many European varieties previously died in infancy, and so this hardy and abundant grapevine became the primary source of American kosher wine.

A distant cousin of European *Vitis vinifera*, the Concord grape (named for the town in Massachusetts, where it was first cultivated) is more suitable for the manufacture of grape jelly than for wine-making. The aroma of wine made from Concord and other *labrusca* grapes is often described as "foxy," a wine term as derogatory as it is vague. "Foxiness," we now know, indicates the presence of certain compounds (methyl anthranilate and o-amino acetophenone) unique to the *labrusca* grapes native to the Eastern seaboard.

"Foxiness" isn't as unpleasant as most wine snobs like to suggest. You might wonder how strange the great European wines would taste to palates honed on centuries of refined *labrusca* viticulture, if such a thing existed. But North America is without such a tradition, and so the early Jewish immigrants in and around New York City fashioned an acceptable wine from the local vines by mitigating Concord's rank grapiness and enamel-stripping acidity with liberal doses of sugar.

Thus, after a few generations, this has become the accepted traditional style of kosher wine in America. And although many wines in the world could be made as kosher for Passover, the sweet and "foxy" fruit of the Concord vine, more akin to cough syrup than to fine wine, remains a sentimental favorite among Jewish Americans.

Other Types of Kosher Wine

Kosher wine doesn't have to be made from the native North American Concord grape that has become such a part of Jewish tradition. Today, Kosher wines are made in California, France, Italy, and Israel, using "normal" wine grapes like the Cabernet Sauvignon and Chenin Blanc. The history of ceremonial wine in all cultures is one rich in red wine, with little or no attention paid to whites. That is still true today, but Kosher whites do exist. The best introduction to good Kosher wines are the Baron Herzog wines from California. They are good and widely available (by Kosher wine standards).

The Kedem winery in upstate New York still produces Concord grape–based Kosher wines. If you want a traditional red Concord wine that doesn't have sugar added to it, look for the Kedem Concord Natural. If you are looking for a very sweet wine, maybe for children, then Kedem Malaga is a logical choice.

Chapter 3

How Is Wine Made?

ALTHOUGH WINEMAKING HAS been raised to a fine art and an increasingly precise science over the last five thousand years, it remains, in essence, a relatively simple process. Wine grapes, *Vitis vinifera*, can grow with considerable ease in most warm-to-temperate climates. Ripe grapes contain a solution of natural sugar and water, with more sugar than in most other fruits. Additionally, the skin of the grape is an ideal medium for the accumulation of natural yeasts. These one-celled plants consume the natural sugar and convert it to ethyl alcohol and carbon dioxide, which, as it escapes the fermenting vat, protects the must from harmful oxidation. Had we not evolved into humans, it's almost conceivable that apes could have learned to make wine—it's that simple. Of course, in the thousands of years since this process was first observed, technology has played an ever-increasing role in winemaking.

There are many technological options available to the modern winemaker. Equipment such as crushers, destemmers, and fermentation tanks come in so many shapes and varieties that each and every winery in the world might well have a unique configuration of them. However, whether the end product is red, white, or pink, and whether it is cheap or expensive, there are several principles common to all winemaking.

Combating Oxidation

First of all, air is the enemy. Exposure to oxygen robs wine of its fresh-tasting qualities and also encourages the activity of acetobacter, the naturally occurring microbes that consume ethyl alcohol and eventually convert it into acetic acid (vinegar). It is an ironic twist of nature that while grapes virtually seek to become wine, wine in turn aspires to become vinegar—again, with minimal effort. The winemaker, therefore, must take care to prevent air from ruining the wine. These precautions begin in the fields at harvest time.

It is crucial that the grapes are picked and transported to the winery without prematurely splitting the skins. While handpicking is best, mechanical harvesting machines have been developed, and these can handle grape bunches with sufficient care. A judicious sprinkling of powdered sulfur dioxide ("sulfite"), an effective antioxidant, is often applied to protect harvested grapes on their way to the winery.

Exposure to air is also minimized during fermentation, and nature lends a helping hand in this stage of winemaking. The carbon dioxide that is discharged by the yeasts, along with ethyl alcohol, provides a cushion of protection against the ambient air. This is especially important in the fermentation of red wine, which usually takes place in an open vat.

As a final precaution against the ill effects of exposure to air, many inexpensive wines are pasteurized—that is, heated to a high-enough temperature to kill the acetobacter. This is an effective way at least to delay the effects of oxidation, and it is the reason why jug wines enjoy such a long shelf life after opening. Inevitably, however, if the wine is kept too long, a new wave of acetobacter will find its way into the wine and begin the process of vinegar-making once again. Because pasteurization is a harsh process that prevents the long-term evolution of wine in the bottle (some oxidation is actually beneficial), this process is rarely used for high-quality wines. A famous exception is Château Corton-Grancey, a *grand cru* red from France's Burgundy region.

Through the Glass, Clearly

Clarity is another goal common to all winemaking, and the brilliant transparency of both red and white wines does not come naturally. Wine is, by nature, cloudy with dead yeast and tiny particulate matter. Several processes, including fining, centrifuging, filtration, racking, and cold stabilization, may be used to clarify wine.

Fining

Fining is one of the few processes in which foreign matter is introduced into the wine. Whipped egg whites have long been used as a fining agent for quality wines. Shortly after fermentation is complete, the wine is transferred to a large settling tank. When added to the tank of young, unfinished wine, the mass of whipped egg whites slowly sinks to the bottom, electrostatically attracting undesirable particles along the way. The clear wine is then drawn off, leaving the coagulated meringue at the bottom of the barrel. In addition to egg whites, casein (milk protein) and bentonite clay (aluminum silicate) can also be used as fining agents.

Centrifuging and Filtration

These are two quick and effective methods of clarifying wine. To centrifuge wine, a container of unfinished, cloudy wine is rapidly rotated so that heavy particles are separated from the wine by centrifugal force. Unfortunately, this process tends to strip wine of some desirable qualities as well, and centrifuging is being used less and less frequently for quality wines. Filtration is the simple and straightforward process of screening out unwanted particles from the wine by passing it through layers of filter paper or synthetic fiber mesh. Though less harsh than centrifuging, there are some fine wines with the term "unfiltered" on the label—the implication being that filtration also strips wine of some desirable qualities.

Racking

Compared to fining, centrifuging, and filtrating, the process of racking is a relatively passive means of clarifying wine. Racking works for the same reason as centrifuging: Unwanted particles are heavier than the wine itself and will eventually sink to the bottom if the wine is left undisturbed. The clear wine can then be "racked," that is, drawn off to another barrel. Again, air is the enemy, and unwanted exposure to air during the racking process must be avoided. Red wines in particular, which are often held for many months in the barrel prior to bottling, may undergo multiple rackings.

Cold Stabilization

This is a relatively harsh treatment used to clarify inexpensive wines. This process involves chilling a tank of wine almost to the freezing point. At this low temperature, minerals such as potassium tartrate (cream of tartar) become less soluble and precipitate out as crystals. Have you ever seen "wine crystals" on a cork? Though often mistaken for unwanted sediment, this accumulation of wine crystals is actually a good sign—it means that the wine has not been cold-stabilized, which would have eliminated the crystals prior to bottling.

Differences Between White Wine and Red Wine Production

Although the prevention of oxidation and some process of clarification are common to all winemaking, there are fundamental differences between the production of red wine and that of white wine. In short, white wine is fermented grape juice—that is, the juice is extracted from the grapes prior to fermentation. Red wine, however, is the juice of fermented grapes, which are crushed into a thick mush—the "must"—from which the juice is extracted after fermentation. Interestingly, the finest rosés are often produced from red grapes handled like white grapes: The red grape skins, which provide color, are removed prior to fermentation, leaving only a slight blush of color in the wine.

The differences between the production of red wine and that of white wine begin in the vineyards. Most of the classic red-wine grape varieties—for example, Cabernet Sauvignon, Merlot, and Syrah— thrive in climates warmer than those that are ideal for the important white-wine varieties. Full ripeness is so crucial for red-wine grapes because the essential components of quality red wine—rich fruit flavors, tannin, body, and color—develop in the grape in the final stage of ripening. However, these grapes must not ripen too quickly. If that happens, the resulting wine often lacks depth and harmony of flavors. The longer the growing season, the more complex the wine, and a prolonged growing season that doesn't bring the grapes to full ripeness until early autumn is ideal. Although most of sunny California's vineyards are planted in the warm valleys, the finest California reds usually come from grapes grown on the cooler slopes overlooking the valleys.

High-quality red and white grapes can often grow side by side, but in general the important white varieties perform best in climates too cool for great reds. Chardonnay, Sauvignon Blanc, and especially Riesling grapes tend to make uninteresting, low-acid wines in the same climates in which the great red grapes may thrive. But Chardonnay is made into the great white wine of the chilly Chablis region of France, an area whose red grapes rarely mature fully. Germany's Rieslings are among the finest wines in the world, yet German red wines are of little more than curiosity value. Riesling, along with an increasing amount of Chardonnay, have been the only *vitis vinifera* varieties that regularly succeed in upstate New York where winter can be brutally cold.

Although the climates in which red- and white-wine grapes thrive may vary, the cultivation techniques are not very different. The real differences between red and white wine production begin after harvest.

White Wine

As soon as possible after picking, white-wine grapes are fed into a crushing and/or destemming machine that gently splits the skins. For most white wines, prolonged skin contact after crushing is not desirable, so the skins and other grape matter are quickly separated from the juice. However, in making some of the great white wines of the world, the skins are allowed to remain in the juice for a day or so in order to lend additional body and character to the wine. A juicing machine uses pressurized sulfur dioxide gas to squeeze out the juice, which then goes to a settling tank, where undesirable solids such as dirt and seeds settle to the bottom. The juice might be centrifuged at this stage, but, as previously mentioned, the centrifuge can remove the good with the bad. The clarified white grape juice is now ready for fermentation . . . well, almost.

Some doctoring of the grape juice might be deemed necessary by the winemaker. Although regulations vary around the world, adjustments in acid and sugar levels are often called for. In cooler regions where even white-wine grape varieties struggle to achieve full ripeness, sugar may be added to the juice, through a process called "chaptalization." Without enough sugar, the wine might not attain the desired alcohol level. Fully ripened grapes usually ferment to an alcohol content of 12 percent by volume. The acidity might also be adjusted at this point. Calcium carbonate may be added to reduce acidity, whereas tartaric or other acids may be added to raise it. In the final analysis, the sugar and acid must be in balance at the desired levels in order to make good wine. Now fermentation can begin.

Fermentation: Grapes Become Wine

Although wild wine yeast naturally accumulates on grape skins during the growing season, almost all winemakers prefer to control fermentation and, therefore, introduce carefully cultivated yeast to the juice. Fermentation proceeds—slowly, it is hoped—because a rapid fermentation might raise the temperature to a level that kills the yeast. Also, the yeast itself imparts character to the wine, so a slow fermentation, which allows longer contact with the yeast, is desirable. Most winemakers control the temperature of the fermentation by refrigeration and recirculation. The carbon dioxide that is produced during fermentation is permitted to escape from the enclosed vat without allowing ambient air back in—yet another precaution against oxidation.

Through this process, the white grape juice has become white wine—rough, unfinished wine that still needs some tinkering, including a filtration to remove any remaining sugar and particles. Just prior to fining, the winemaker may deem it necessary to add some sweet, unfermented grape juice in which the yeasts and acetobacters have been killed. This is done to add roundness to the flavor and to take the acidic edge off a harsh-tasting wine. However, the new wine has its own way of reducing its acidity: malolactic fermentation.

This process, like alcoholic fermentation, occurs naturally but is usually controlled by the winemaker. In the spring following the harvest, warm weather activates microbes in the wine that convert malic acid into lactic acid and carbon dioxide. Malic acid, which is naturally present in apples, is sharply acidic. Lactic acid, which develops naturally in dairy products, is only half as acidic as malic acid. Thus, malolactic fermentation softens a wine's acidity profile. This process can be controlled by the winemaker to such a degree that you can find a range of wines in the market that have undergone various degrees of malolactic fermentation: from clean, crisp white wines that have not undergone any malolactic fermentation; to soft, fleshy white wines that have undergone full malolactic fermentation; to wines somewhere in the middle, a blend of wines made in the two different styles. Some wines have been known to undergo an unintended malolactic fermentation after bottling, resulting in a funny-tasting wine with an unwelcome trace of fizziness.

A Hint or More of Oak

Up until a few decades ago, oak casks were the most economical storage vessels available. Oak imparts distinct flavors to a wine, mainly vanilla and tannin. These flavors are more apparent in white wines than in heavier, more complex reds. Because of the long history of wine storage in oak, these flavors have become accepted as basic components of wine. It is even likely that the style of certain wines, notably the Chardonnay-based white Burgundy wines, evolved in such a way that oak flavors are a necessary and expected facet of the wine's flavor; without oak, such wines might taste incomplete. Now that less expensive storage vessels are available, such as those made of stainless steel, oak flavor is an additive of sorts. In fact, some producers of inexpensive wines circumvent the great expense of oak barrels by adding oak chips to wine held in stainless-steel tanks.

Virtually all wines benefit from a resting period after fermentation and clarification. A few months of aging, either in oak or steel, allows the flavor components in white wine to become more harmonious. Likewise, a resting period in the bottle is beneficial. An unfortunate consequence of the wine boom is that most wines are consumed long before they are at their best. Although red wines generally undergo a much more gradual evolution in the bottle than do white wines, a well-made white wine can improve for five or more years in the bottle. Chardonnays and Rieslings are known to age more gracefully than other white wines.

Red Wine

Red wine is not necessarily "better" than white wine, but well-made red wines have more flavor components and, thus, are typically more complex than white wines. Enjoyable white wine has a prominent acidity profile counterbalanced with a hint of sweetness, restrained fruit flavors, and maybe a touch of oak. That is why white wines are best served chilled—acidic beverages, such as lemonade, taste better at lower temperatures. If served warm, both lemonade and white wine are less enjoyable because the prominent acidity becomes unpleasantly sharp at higher temperatures. Although red wine may be nearly as acidic as white, red wine usually has a wider range of fruit flavors as well as a noticeable amount of tannin, qualities best appreciated at warmer temperatures. The difference is skin deep.

Whereas (almost) all grapes contain the same greenish pulp, the skins of red-wine grapes give red wine its color, tannins, and assorted fruit flavors. So white grape skins, which add little to white wine, are removed early in the winemaking process, but red grape skins are kept in the fermenting vat for an extended period of time. It is, therefore, necessary to remove the stalks from red-wine grapes as they are crushed, lest the stalks impart excessive tannins on the wine. "Tannins"—the family of organic acids present in grape skins as well as seeds—cause the dry and bitter sensation in your mouth after you bite a grape seed.

The image of half-naked men stomping grapes in an open vat is familiar to many of us. Although technology has replaced the human foot in most corners of the wine world, the open vat is still widely used for red-wine production because grape skins tend to rise to the top of the fermenting must, forming a "cap" atop the juice. In order to extract the desirable qualities from the skins, this cap must be continuously mixed back into the juice. This can be accomplished by pumping juice from the bottom of the barrel over the cap (called "pumping over") or by manually punching the cap back into the juice with a special paddle (called "punched-cap fermentation"). It is said that a punched-cap wine reflects the physical character of the wine-maker—a big, strong winemaker will force more extract from the skins, resulting in a big, strong wine. As in white-wine production, temperature control is important, though red wines benefit from a fermentation temperature a little higher than that which is ideal for whites.

Drawing off the Wine

After fermentation is complete, perhaps one to three weeks later, the new wine is drawn from the fermenting vat, leaving the skins behind. This first run of juice, called "free-run" juice, comes forth voluntarily; forcibly squeezing the juice from the must would extract excessive tannin. Only after the free-run juice is removed is the remaining must squeezed, yielding "press wine," a portion of which might be blended with the free-run juice in order to adjust the tannin level carefully. The wine is then clarified in much the same manner as white wine and transferred to aging barrels, where it can slowly mature. Racking may be necessary every few months if the wine is held in the cellar for a length of time. Prolonged barrel aging before bottling is desirable for most types of red wine, since the broad array of flavor components generally needs more time to harmonize in red wines than in white wines.

Many wines, both red and white, are blends of several different grapes. Even in the case of wines made entirely from one variety, a winemaker may blend different "lots" (separate barrels) of wine in order to make the best possible wine. The "recipe" for such wines may vary from year to year, depending on the characteristics of the available lots in a given vintage.

When wine is deemed ready for release, it is transferred to bot-tles in a mechanized process notable for its sanitation. Once again, air is the enemy, and care is taken not to allow its contact with the wine during bottling. Germs and impurities are also mortal enemies, and the bottling process is often the most highly mechanized step in the entire operation, as sparkling-clean bottles are filled, corked, capped, and labeled with minimal human contact. For the finest wines it is often advantageous for the winery to then keep the bottles in storage for two or more years. This makes for better wine when it finally reaches the market, and in many cases the value of the wine will have increased greatly during its slumber.

Part 2

Why We Love Wine

Chapter 4

What Makes Good Wine Good?

HOW CAN YOU TELL if wine is good? To paraphrase Duke Ellington, if it tastes good, it is good . . . Alas, the "experts" out there have a near-monopoly in deciding what is good and what is not, but you can certainly decide for yourself what you like. As you learn more and more about wine, you will develop confidence in your own taste, and you will be able to taste a wine and know immediately if you like it or not. Furthermore, even if you don't exactly love a particular wine, you will be able to tell whether or not it is nonetheless a good, well-made wine. It might very well be that certain wines suit someone else's style, but not yours. To best illustrate the characteristics of quality wines, let's take a hypothetical look at a few "perfect" glasses of wine.

Wine #1: White Served at 45°–50°F

The first quality we notice is crystalline clarity—this wine is like a liquid diamond! The initial sniff fills our heads with aromas of wet stones, ripe peaches, and lime rinds. The first sip is so bracingly acidic that it is hard to comprehend fully. Then the second sip brings the flavors into sharp focus and reveals layer upon layer of fruit and mineral elements, along with bright, mouth-watering acidity perfectly balanced by a hint of sweetness. The flavors practically dance on your tongue and seem to last forever. This is what great Riesling from one of Germany's finest regions tastes like.

Wine #2: Red Served at 55°–60°F

The glass of red, served about 10° or 15° warmer than the white, is its opposite in many ways. Unlike the crystal-clear white, the deep, purplish-black color of this wine is nearly opaque. Clearly, it is a densely flavored wine. Upon sniffing this wine, ripe aromas of blackberry and cassis greet your nose, along with a slight whiff of cedar and mint. This is a massive wine, and after just a small sip, your mouth is immediately flooded with these powerful fruit flavors, as well as a silky and detailed tannic structure, which provides just enough "grip" in your mouth.

There's no dancing here—this wine is too heavy and complex for that. Rather, you are carried away by the engaging array of heady textures, flavors, and aromas that remain in your mouth and memory long after swallowing each sip. This sort of heavenly red wine illustrates the greatness that Californian sunshine can coax from the Cabernet Sauvignon grape.

The Self-Fulfilling Prophesy of Perfection

Two wines, opposites in many ways, yet both are "perfect." What do they have in common? For starters, they were both meant to be great. Just as the Ford Taurus is a perfectly good car that will never win the Indianapolis 500, there are mass-produced but well-made wines on the market that are meant for nothing more than casual, everyday consumption. "Everyday" wine will never be mistaken for world-class wine. However, the two wines described above were meant to be great, and great care was taken to make them so.

Great wine is, in a way, a self-fulfilling prophesy. Knowing that his wine traditionally commands top price, a wine producer can justify a "spare no expense" approach in the vineyard and cellar. For instance, it is said that great wine is grown, not made, and no vineyard decision affects the quality of the final product as does the crop level, expressed in *tons per acre*. A typical Napa Valley Cabernet vineyard might be capable of ripening, say, five tons per acre, but a quality-conscious grower might decide to thin the crop so as to yield less than half that amount. By doing so, he is rewarded with exceptionally ripe grapes that yield a more richly textured and correspondingly pricier wine than if he had reaped and vinified the maximum crop.

Wooden aging barrels, once an absolute necessity for wine production, are now something of a luxury item. For most of the world's wine, the stainless-steel tank is a perfectly good place for a wine to repose before bottling, and yet the aroma gained from aging in French oak barrels is like expensive perfume. For many of the world's greatest wines, the unmistakable whiff of the French oak barrel is an integral component. These barrels cost about $700 each and thus add about $2.50 to the cost of producing a 750ml bottle of wine. Of course, wine barrels are used for several years, and their expense is thus spread over several vintages. But barrels are only new once, and many pricey wines—both red and white—spend part of their lives in new French oak.

Double the Oak

In its richest vintages, the famous dessert wine Château d'Yquem of Sauternes in Bordeaux is racked from its original new oak barrels into another round of new oak, thus justifying its proud boast of "200 percent new oak"—certainly a worthwhile expense for a $250 bottle. ❧

Producers of less expensive wines employ various shortcuts to add the oak flavor, which has become, for many wine drinkers, an expected component of Chardonnay and other favorite varietal wines. Oak chips, when temporarily steeped in wine in a giant steel vat, can approximate to a somewhat acceptable degree the caramel-like flavor imparted by oak barrels, and this technique is used for many mass-market wines.

Great Grapes

Grape variety is of primary importance in the production of great wine; you cannot usually make a silk purse from a sow's ear, as the saying goes. While a profound wine might occasionally be produced from a pedestrian strain of grapes, the rare exceptions prove the rule: Great wine comes from great grapes. What makes certain grapes great? That's hard to say, except that centuries of experience have taught winemakers and wine lovers which grapes are responsible for the most prized wines.

For example, over the past several centuries, the Cabernet Sauvignon variety has proven to be one of the greatest of the red wine grapes. It is genetically endowed with a thick, flavorful skin and, therefore, requires considerable heat accumulation over the course of the growing season to attain full ripeness. Underripe Cabernet Sauvignon has an unpleasantly weedy, green flavor.

However, when grown to absolutely full ripeness on the sun-drenched hillsides of California or in the gulf stream-warmed Médoc in Bordeaux, the thick skin of the Cabernet Sauvignon grape reliably develops the unique chemical components that are responsible for Cabernet Sauvignon's signature array of flavors and aromas. Similarly, time and experience have shown winemakers in many parts of the world that the Riesling grape, when ripened under its own ideal conditions, yields luscious, crystal-clear, nectar-like white wine with the unique fruit and mineral flavors that we have come to associate with the finest versions.

Other, inferior grapes grown under the same conditions as Cabernet and Riesling may indeed produce good wine, but will rarely equal wine made from these noblest of wine grapes. Of course, there are some great wines produced in wine regions unsuitable for Cabernet Sauvignon or Riesling. Chardonnay and Pinot Noir are arguably the co-equals of Riesling and Cabernet Sauvignon in the royal hierarchy of *Vitis vinifera*. Chardonnay is produced in a wide variety of wine regions around the world, including prime California acreage too warm for Riesling. And the early ripening Pinot Noir becomes royalty-grade red wine in the continental climate of Burgundy, a region too cool for Cabernet Sauvignon.

Different wine grapes prefer different soils. Chardonnay, for instance, may grow in a wide variety of soils but seems to perform best in those with a chalk or limestone component, while Riesling seems quite happy in the slate-rich slopes of the Mosel valley. Among red wine grapes, Cabernet Sauvignon is known to perform well in well-drained soils of varied composition in many different parts of the world, while the more finicky Pinot Noir grape, like Chardonnay, seems to favor limestone-rich soils as in its native Burgundy.

Quantity over Quality?

Far away from the world's prized growing regions are the work-horse vineyards in which *quantity*, not *quality*, is of primary importance. The Languedoc region of Southern France was for many decades the source of nondescript country wine, mass-produced for daily consumption by France's working class. The Aramon grape, now thankfully banished to the history books, reliably yielded over twenty tons of grapes per acre in the Languedoc's relatively fertile loam. Here in America, the great Central Valley of California affords wine grapes the greatest heat accumulation in the Golden State, making it possible to ripen the most marketable varieties (if in name only) at obscenely high crop levels.

Lately, there is some good news from these volume-oriented outposts. France's Languedoc region is having great success with red Rhône varieties when crop levels are held in check. Likewise, Lodi, now a government-recognized quality wine-producing subregion of California's Central Valley, is now beginning to produce some remarkable versions of the heat-loving Zinfandel grape.

The Final Analysis

So, after all, what makes great wine great? In short, the world's greatest wines are usually those that are meant to be great, and recognized as such by the "experts" as well as the wine-buying public. In most (but not all) cases, great wines come from the best grape varieties, grown in the best soil in the world's great wine regions, and are produced by winemakers with the knowledge and desire to produce wines of such a caliber. Attention is paid to every detail, no matter how expensive. The fact that there are unpredictable exceptions to this axiom—surprising wines from unusual grapes or from lesser-known regions—is one of the things that keeps the wine world from becoming boring.

If you're like most people, the thought of savoring a truly "perfect" bottle of wine is an occasional luxury at best, and certainly not an experience to be replicated on a regular basis! Don't worry—there are thousands of wines made all over the world that are not "great" but are perfectly good wines to drink. Some of these, in fact, might even be terrific bargains. One of the keys to a lifetime of wine enjoyment is first learning what the great wines of the world taste like, and then finding inexpensive wines that remind you of them.

Chapter 5

The Quality Spectrum

THE LOCAL WINE STORE might sell wines ranging from $3 to $300. What kind of wine do you get for your money?

Category 1: Jug Wines ($10–$13 per 4-Liter Bottle)

These wines are named for their large bottles. Because they are usually made from blends of lesser grapes, their labels rarely indicate a grape variety. Jug-wine producers from California have traditionally borrowed famous names from Europe, including "Chablis," "Rhine," "Burgundy," "Chianti," and so on. This trend, however, is fading. Look for brand names or simply a labeling of red, white, or rosé. As the price of mass-produced grapes continues to fall, watch for ever-cheaper varietal bottlings in the jug format.

Most Americans know of the chablis (with a small "c")— the light, inexpensive, inoffensive, off-dry (slightly sweet), white jug wine—before they learn of the true, French Chablis, from the eponymous wine village in France. True Chablis can be among the world's best Chardonnays. These wines are labeled Chablis, not Chardonnay, since the European custom is to name wines after regions and not grapes.

The Burgundy region of France produces Pinot Noirs of unsurpassed quality. This has nothing to do with California "burgundy," although they are both red wines. The Chianti district of Italy produces wine made from the Sangiovese grape, and some of these versions are among the world's best red wines. California "chianti" is off-dry, simple red wine, perfectly suitable for spaghetti and meatballs. Finally, Rhine is a German wine region famous for its Rieslings—flowery, off-dry, and complex. California "rhine" is merely white, and may well be sugary-sweet.

These four names cause a great deal of confusion for the novice wine drinker. When the knowledgeable wine consumer hears or reads about one of these four regions, he or she thinks in terms of great quality and great tradition. The American novice, on the other hand, thinks of mass-produced, generic wines. This is just one of the many examples of the wine language barrier that makes entering the wine world difficult.

Despite this misuse of famous European wine place names, California jug wines aren't all that bad. These wines are made to be inexpensive but good tasting—two good qualities in any beverage. In fact, these wines can be an excellent value when the occasion calls for a simple wine.

Category 2: "Fighting" Varietals ($5–$8)

These inexpensive wines are labeled and sold under varietal names—Chardonnay, Merlot, Cabernet Sauvignon, etc., and are "fighting" for the customer's dollar. (The competition is fierce in this category.) Unfortunately, they are often recognizable in name only, as the signature qualities of the grape varieties rarely appear in this price range. This doesn't mean these wines can't taste good; it's just that the good-tasting $7 Merlot might not taste very much like a typical Merlot.

These wines do, of course, comply with labeling laws. However, they are not usually produced from better grape lots of the indicated variety; they instead represent the bottom of the heap. It is also safe to assume that a hefty portion of your wine dollar frequently goes to waste on the varietal name. Suffice it to say that people who demand cheap Chardonnay and Merlot get what they deserve. However, a bargain-rich country like Chile does produce some pretty good Merlot for $7 or $8.

Category 3: Midrange Varietals ($8–$18)

Midrange varietals fill a need in the wine market that went unmet until the mid-1980s—affordable, "good" wines labeled according to grape variety. Like fighting varietals, midrange varietals don't vary much from year to year. The majority of such labeled wines sold in North America come from California. What, then, is different? For a couple of dollars more, you can buy a Chardonnay that is varietally recognizable. These wines are better, perhaps made from slightly more expensive grapes grown in cooler regions, and they allow you to understand what a particular variety of wine is supposed to taste like.

The competition is probably fiercest in this category, perhaps even tougher than in the "fighting varietal" category, which helps the consumer. You're likely to find bargains on one brand or another due to price wars—deep deals on high-quantity purchases at the whole-sale level.

Category 4: Handcrafted Wines ($18–$30)

"Handcrafted" refers to wines made by small ("boutique") wineries where the winemaker enjoys a close, "hands-on" relationship with the wine throughout the winemaking process. Production is typically small, and a producer of handcrafted varietals usually doesn't mind if they sell out of wine in a given year. In contrast, midrange, volume-oriented producers usually have stockholders to satisfy, and selling out of wine would present a business problem. Such wineries have been known to purchase bulk, unfinished wines, even from other countries, and then blend, bottle, and sell it under their own label.

Handcrafted wines also differ from large, midrange producers in terms of consistency from year to year. Whereas the large producer is inclined to strive for a uniform product from each vintage, hand-crafted wines might vary from one vintage to the next because the wine reflects the idiosyncrasies of each vintage.

Category 5: Reserve Wines ($30 and up)

The "reserve" designation, though without legal meaning in the United States, often indicates a wine of greater quality than the winery's regular offering. It usually means that better grapes, or better lots of blending wine, were used in its manufacture. Because the term may be used without legal restriction, the term "reserve" might well appear on an ordinary and inexpensive bottle of wine in the United States.

Vintages

Because wine is an agricultural product that can keep for several years, most quality wines give the year of harvest on the label. Yet, the vintage date is a frequently misunderstood piece of information. The year of harvest tells you two things: how old the wine is, and, because climate conditions vary from year to year, whether or not the wine was produced in a "good year." But a "good" year can be many things: an abundant harvest, a high-quality harvest, or both. Growing conditions might have been excellent in one area but below average in a neighboring area; that's why we call them microclimates. Also, growing conditions might have been terrific for one grape variety but not another. (You'll learn more about climate and growing conditions in Chapter 9, Wine Regions.)

The vintage date, especially for inexpensive wines, can also serve as a "freshness date." Most white and rosé wines are best drunk before their second or third birthday. Even inexpensive red wines are made to be consumed right away rather than aged for several years. It is a truism yet to be refuted that red wine is either enjoyable in its youth or enjoyable in full maturity, but not both. On the other hand, Great Chardonnays, especially those from Burgundy (France) can improve for several years in the bottle, as can sweet dessert white wines. Aside from these exceptions, younger is probably better for inexpensive wines.

Some Years Are Better Than Others

For the great wines of the world, some years are much better than others. There are many different regions in the world that produce great red wine. However, until recently, a "good year" meant a good year for red wine in Bordeaux, France, where 1961 was regarded as "the vintage of the century." And a unique year it was. The grape crop in Bordeaux was nearly destroyed by bad weather early in the season, but a gorgeous summer ripened the remaining grapes to perfection. Thus, the 1961 Bordeaux reds were both superb and scarce. Forty-three years later, some of them are still improving in the bottle.

The Value of Vintage Dates

The bottom line is, unless you are shopping for expensive wine of the "vintage-sensitive" type—Piedmontese and Tuscan red wines from Italy, Red Bordeaux, or Red and White Burgundy—do not place too much stock in the vintage date. But do be sure to use the vintage date to make sure that the wine you are buying is still young enough to enjoy as it was intended to be. ❧

1964 was a split-personality year in Bordeaux. In Pomerol and Saint Emilion, where the earlier ripening Merlot grape predominates, the wines were outstanding. However, across the river in Médoc and Graves, heavy rains fell before the Cabernet Sauvignon was harvested, and the Cabernet Sauvignon–based wines from these districts were rather thin. It is likewise true in California that the quality of a vintage can vary somewhat from one microclimate to another, and from one grape variety to another.

California has remarkably consistent growing weather and "bad years" just don't seem to happen. Some years, however, have been better than others, and there has recently been a succession of very good years beginning in 1990.

What Makes Expensive Wines Expensive?

An expensive wine doesn't start out the same way ordinary wine does. By this we mean that it isn't discovered, nor does it develop by chance. It is expensive to make, and it is made to be expensive.

Good Vineyards Don't Come Cheap

The best grapes grow in the best vineyards. The best vineyards don't have the most fertile soil, but they do have the best soil for growing wine grapes. These soils pass on elements of mineral flavor to the grapes, and thus to the wine. These vineyards also have good climates for growing wine grapes. The concept of microclimate is very important in the wine world. The amount of sun and cooling breezes can vary considerably from acre to acre in areas with hilly terrain.

These differences contribute to differences in grape flavors. The better the vineyard, the more expensive the land. Vineyards worthy of individual recognition are few in number, so the cost associated with a limited resource that is in high demand certainly comes into play. Unlike the contrived scarcity of diamonds, the scarcity of top vineyard acreage is quite real.

The Value of the Vines

In addition to the vineyard factor, there is also the vine factor to consider. Older vines produce fewer but better grapes. So it is more expensive to have older vines in the ground because they yield fewer bottles. Some wine labels that claim old vines are stretching the truth. There is no accepted standard as to just what constitutes "old vines."

Superior Juice

All grape juice isn't created equal. The best wines are made from the best juice. This juice costs more than lesser juice, especially when it is bought on the open market. Free-run juices come from grapes that are lightly crushed or allowed to crush themselves under their own weight. Often grapes whose best juice has been drained off are then more thoroughly crushed. That juice is used for lesser wines.

Roll out the Best Barrels

The top juice is often put into the best oak barrels that money can buy—those made from French Limousin Oak. A new oak barrel can add a dollar or more to the cost of producing each bottle of wine from that barrel. After the best juice is allowed to ferment and/or age in the best barrels, the winemaker comes along and chooses the best of the best to be his top wine. The rest of the best will probably become the second-string wine, which is still going to be very good and quite expensive, but not the *best*.

The Cost of Aging

Many top wines are crafted to be aged many years to bring out the best a grape has to offer. This cellar aging in a barrel or a bottle certainly doesn't help cash flow. This, therefore, is another factor in pricing. ❧

Top wines from top winemakers have a loyal following that supports the pricing of these wines. If the quality falls off, then these winemakers lose the necessary buyers. They can't afford to cut quality, even if it means producing far fewer bottles of these expensive wines in an off year. Some of these top wines might not be produced at all in some years, yet much of the cost is still incurred.

Why Expensive Wines Are Worth It

If you've ever been to a good wine store, you probably have looked at the expensive wines and wondered a few things. The biggest puzzle to you might be why anyone would spend hundreds of dollars for a bottle of wine.

Getting a wine neophyte to understand this practice is like trying to get an atheist to believe in God. It takes a leap of faith. If you have never tasted a good $20 bottle, the leap to a $100 bottle is gigantic. Think of it as listening to an orchestra performance in person at symphony hall, versus listening to the same music on your home stereo. Going from a $10 bottle to a $20 bottle is like buying better speakers for your stereo. When you get to a certain level of wine quality, buying a great wine becomes like buying tickets to a live performance.

More Isn't Necessarily Better

However, just because the music sounds better doesn't mean you will enjoy it any more. The same is true for wine. Just because you are drinking a better wine, it doesn't mean you are going to enjoy the wine-drinking experience more. If you love music, you know that just being able to listen to your favorite song on any music system can be one of life's most enjoyable experiences.

Just as there are a lot of expectations when you go to the symphony, there are also a lot of expectations when you pull the cork on a $100 bottle of wine. It is hard to enjoy anything in life if you aren't relaxed, receptive, and prepared to enjoy it to the fullest.

Now that we all feel good about not being able to justify spending $100 on a bottle of wine, let's talk more about such precious bottles. In April 1984, I sat with my roommate in our $180-per-month college apartment and drank a $150 bottle of wine. It was La Tache 1978, a Pinot Noir from France's Burgundy region.

Was this wine worth the money? Wine like this is certainly a luxury item, and six $25 bottles might make more sense to you. Or maybe even six $10 bottles and a great new spring jacket might seem like a wiser use of $150. But we both enjoyed that bottle more than any other bottle of wine we have ever had. Two factors made this wine-drinking experience so phenomenal. (Actually three, if you count the fact that neither of us had to pay for the wine.)

The first factor was the startling evolution of the wine during the sixty minutes from the time we opened the bottle until the last delicious mouthful. Upon opening the bottle, the wine tasted quite harsh, as if it had gone bad in the bottle. But after five minutes, the flavors snapped into focus. It was as if the flavors changed dramatically every ten minutes or so. The experience in its entirety was like tasting five or six very good wines.

The second factor was the flavor (or flavors!) of the wine itself. A gentle framework of soft tannins with an overlay of a fleshy, mouth-filling, glycerine body supported a palette of nuances—raspberry, cherry, smoke, coffee, and soil, among others. And the flavors lingered in the mouth.

Good wines have structure (firmness without harshness); balanced components (so the wine isn't "too" anything); complexity in the mouth (so they thoroughly stimulate the taste buds on both a sensual and an intellectual level); and body (not too thick, not too thin)—and they taste good. A great wine does all of these things, but it is the level of balanced complexity in its flavors and components that puts it into a different league, a league most people will never know exists (and may not ever care to know).

A Complex Medley

Sticking with the music analogy, let's take a shot at this complexity thing. Think of the components of a good wine as if they were the instruments in a six-piece ensemble. Maybe you can pick out the violin, the cello, and the other instruments while you listen to and enjoy the music, both as a total entity and as individual entities.

When you have a symphony orchestra, you up the ante. Rather than one violin, there are many violins. This gives the music a fuller sound, and it adds a thickness to it. It's like going from a two-dimensional world to a three-dimensional world. The violin section plays as one, yet the sound is quite different from that of a single violin. It has an underlying richness. It's the difference between a square and a cube. That is why large orchestras exist. A great wine is like a great orchestra, with its components having a thickness of dimension, a thickness that can be better savored than described.

Chapter 6

Wine Flaws

WINE IS A NEARLY NATURAL PRODUCT produced by humans. As such, it is bound to have a few imperfections. When wine turned bad in Ancient Rome, the Romans added everything from milk to mustard to their wine in order to mask its flaws. The following is a summary of the most common wine flaws. Some of them are curable; others are not. (Hold the mustard.)

The Wine Is Too Old

As you've already learned earlier in this book, all wines go through an aging process. Some wines, such as Beaujolais Nouveau, are made to be drunk in their infancy and contain almost none of the components that prolong their life in the bottle. At the other end of the spectrum, certain wines, such as expensive Bordeaux and port, are vinified so as to improve in the bottle for as long as half a century. All other wines fall somewhere in between these two extremes.

Whether it is Beaujolais or Bordeaux, wine rarely spoils in the way that old food does because the relatively high acidity in wine prevents most (although not all) bacterial spoilage. That said, no wine can last forever, and wine that is past its prime is usually characterized by a lack of fruity aromas and flavors ("dried out") and, perhaps, a degree of oxidation.

There is little that can be done to improve over-the-hill wine. If you have a pretty good bottle of wine that has obviously seen better days, you would be wise to drink it quickly after opening because it will probably not improve with prolonged exposure to air.

Among popular red wines today, a ten-year-old Californian Cabernet Sauvignon is probably a safer choice than a Californian Pinot Noir of the same vintage. You can generally assume that a red wine from the Old World (France or Italy) is meant to age more reliably than a New-World red.

The Wine Is Too Young

We should all have such problems!

It is generally regarded in knowledgeable wine circles as infanticide to drink a young vintage of fabulous (and pricey) wine that is obviously vinified to improve with age for many years. Wine that is too young can often be identified by the "next day test." Open a bottle and drink, say, two glasses of it with your dinner; if the remainder tastes even better the next day, then the wine will probably improve with some aging.

If you are knowingly serving a red wine that is way too young, you can duplicate one aspect of the maturation process by exposing it to air for a few hours before serving. This is best done by vigorously pouring the wine into a large (one liter) glass carafe, pouring it back into the bottle with a funnel, and then back into the carafe. If done a few hours before serving, the exposure to the air will soften the young wine's tannins and allow the fruit aromas to open up.

Most customers drink their wines on the day of their purchase. When, say, a highly rated Cabernet Sauvignon from a recent vintage is released, it quickly disappears from the retail shelves and customers tend to drink them long before they should. Buying such treasures by the case will not only get you a discount, it will also reward you with a handsome return on your investment if you resist the temptation to open the box for a year.

The Wine Is Carsick

You read the glowing review, and you bought the wine as soon as it hit your retailer's shelf. Now you've opened it for a fancy dinner party with your boss, and the wine is nowhere near as good as it should be. What happened?

Wine doesn't like to travel any more than small children do. After a month-long voyage at sea and perhaps a train ride, fine wines may seem disjointed and out-of-balance if consumed right away. Dramamine won't help, but a month or so of rest will.

The Wine Is Poorly Made

This category of flaws might seem rather broad, but it's certainly worthy of mention because it is possible for winemakers to make conscious decisions in the wine cellar that lead to glaring imperfections in their wines. For instance, in marginal regions where the Chardonnay has difficulty attaining full ripeness—the Northeastern

United States comes to mind here, for instance—enthusiastic wine-makers sometimes rely too heavily on new French oak, using it like makeup to mask a wine's mediocrity rather than to enhance its natural beauty. Therefore, you might exercise caution when buying "reserve" Chardonnays, because their higher price might simply be footing the winery's hefty lumber tab.

Also, some winemakers take great pride in producing "unfiltered" wines, and there are some excellent examples out there. "Unfiltered" wines are not inherently better than "filtered" wines, yet the term appears on many wine labels with the implication that unfiltered wines are somehow superior. Filtration removes both particulate material from the wine as well as microorganisms that can lead to spoilage, and therefore "unfiltered" wines can turn bad more easily and show more bottle variation (not a good thing) than their filtered counterparts.

The Wine Is out of Balance

The various flavor components that make up a wine—fruity esters, tannins, acidity, alcohol, and oak—should ideally come together in perfect harmony. If they don't, then the result is wine that's out of balance. For example, wine that is too tannic is hard on the mouth, kind of like biting into a wool sweater. In this case, exposure to air will help to make this sort of wine seem softer. Imbalance can also occur with big, powerful reds that sometimes go through a "dumb" phase, during which the wine's fruit flavors are buried beneath the tannins. If this is the case, additional aging might help. Wine that is too warm or too cold might also display disjointed, unbalanced flavors. (See the following section.)

The Wine Is the Wrong Temperature

The temperature at which a wine is served can make a tremendous difference in consumption, and different wines require different temperatures to achieve their fullest potential. For example, it is difficult to appreciate white wine fully if it is too cold, because the fruity flavors in an overchilled wine are numbed by the cold. Consequently, you will notice that many subtle flavors emerge from hiding as the wine warms up in your glass. On the other hand, white wine that is too warm will seem sharply acidic and in this case should be returned to the ice bucket to chill for a few minutes. In any case, white wine should generally be served slightly warmer than refrigerator temperature, at least 45°F. Sparkling wine is most enjoyable at a slightly cooler temperature.

Overchilled red wine will seem angular and harsh in your mouth because the tannins are far more apparent at lower temperatures. If red wine is too warm, however, it will seem hot in your mouth because the alcohol is more volatile at these higher temperatures. When serving red wine, especially during the summer months, it is important to be mindful of its serving temperature. A 75° dining room, especially one that is air-conditioned to a low level of humidity, is perfectly comfortable in the hot summer months, but it is much too warm for red wine. Keep in mind that the "serve red wine at room temperature" rule was perhaps written when rooms were kept at a brisk 60°. Therefore, it is generally a good idea to immerse red wines in a bucket of cold tap water for a few minutes before serving. Red wines low in tannin, such as Beaujolais and Pinot Noir, are enjoyable at cooler temperatures than are full-bodied, tannic reds.

The Wine Is "Corked"

Have you ever opened a bottle of expensive wine with great anticipation, only to be greeted by a musty whiff of wet cardboard? If so, you are a victim of "cork taint," and you are not alone. It is estimated that perhaps 5 percent of all bottles suffer from this flaw. This problem arises because wine corks are treated with a mild chlorine solution, which can react with naturally occurring phenol compounds in the cork. This reaction produces trichlorophenol, which is in turn transformed by moisture-loving molds into trichloranisole, or TCA, the ultimate source of the "corked" aroma.

TCA is detectable by experienced noses in parts per *trillion*, and yet many wine customers unknowingly drink corked bottles, perhaps because the "corkiness" often blends in with the woody flavors in some wines. Whether you've ordered wine in a restaurant or purchased it from a retail store, if you suspect cork taint you should definitely ask for another bottle. Because of the escalating cost of cork taint to the wine industry each year, there is a growing movement toward the use of the screwcap closure, which will completely eliminate the problem.

The Wine Is Oxidized

Remember that for the most part oxygen is wine's enemy. Wine that suffers from excessive exposure to air will have a slightly burnt, sherry-like aroma and flavor. In small doses this might be a pleasant nuance if the wine is complex and well-aged; in fact, some of the fortified wines, such as sherry, madeira, and marsala, rely on a degree of oxidation in their production. A little oxidation goes a long way, however, and it is generally considered a fault in table wines. If a wine is harboring any acetobacter, the microbe responsible for vinegar production, exposure to oxygen can have dire consequences. In the presence of oxygen, the acetobacter proceed with their malevolent task, first by converting ethyl alcohol to acetaldehyde and then into acetic acid, the primary component of vinegar. Ethyl acetate, a related by-product of oxidation in wine, smells like nail polish and frequently shows up when wine has been left open for too long. This is often the case in restaurants when they offer a wide variety of wines by the glass without an adequate preservation system.

The Wine Is "Bretty"

Certain red wines, such as red burgundies and chiantis, are often described as having a "barnyard aroma." This particular trait is often desirable in small doses but is considered a flaw when it dominates the flavor of a wine. "Brett" is shorthand for *brettanomyces*, a spoilage yeast that grows naturally on grape skins. Excessively bretty wines are more often than not the result of less-than-pristine hygienic practices in the winery's cellar.

The Wine Is Fizzy

The delightful froth in champagnes and sparkling wines is caused by the presence of dissolved carbon dioxide. Still (nonsparkling) wines sometimes develop a trace or more of fizziness, and this is usually (but not always) a flaw. If a winemaker fails to remove all of the yeast cells before bottling, those that remain might resume their work on the residual sugar in the wine. This results in a little more alcohol production and a prickle of carbonation. Likewise, a winemaker might bottle wine that is still susceptible to a malo-lactic fermentation, by which lactic bacteria converts harsh malic acid into milder lactic acid and carbon dioxide.

There are exceptions where a slight fizziness is actually beneficial in nonsparkling wines, and some youthful whites, particularly German Rieslings and Italian Pinot Grigios, sport a fine prickle that emphasizes the young wine's freshness. Young reds, particularly Pinot Noir, may also "wink at the brim" immediately after opening. You'll be able to recognize when this sort of mild carbonation is acceptable in young wines because it usually blows off after a few minutes. If not, however, you should consider it a flaw in the wine.

The Wine Is Cloudy

Generally, wine should be more or less clear. This holds true for all sorts of wines, from German Riesling, which should be clear like a liquid crystal, to full-bodied reds, which, while often dense, should still be clear around the rim of the glass. Wine can be clarified through several different processes including fining, filtering, centrifuging, and racking.

"Fining" involves adding some foreign material such as beaten egg whites or bentonite clay to a vat wine. These substances electrostatically attract particulate matter as it settles to the bottom. After fining, clear wine is carefully drawn off from the fining agent and the particles, in a process known as "racking." Unfined and unfiltered wine is usually clarified by racking after a period in which the particulates and/or dead yeast settle in the barrel's belly.

Still other wines are clarified by spinning them in containers so that the solids separate by centrifugal force. Wine that is noticeably cloudy has either not been properly clarified or is suffering from post-bottling biological activity due to bacteria or yeast cells. If you encounter a bottle of wine such as this, enjoy at your own risk.

Stuff Has Settled on the Bottom

Well-aged reds often "throw sediment," which means they might gradually develop a deposit of solids at the bottom of the bottle. Such wines should be carefully decanted (a process virtually identical to racking) before serving. Failure to decant crusted wines properly can result in cloudiness as well as a Turkish coffee-like sludge in the last few sips. Wines not subjected to the harsh process of cold stabilization might develop "wine crystals," another type of deposit found in the bottom of white wines and usually stuck to the corks of red wines. There's no need to be overly concerned about this, however. These flavorless tartrate precipitates will not redissolve into the wine and thus do not significantly affect the enjoyment of wine.

The Wine Is Too Expensive

Last but certainly not least . . . the price of wine is by far the most common flaw of all! There is an ocean of good wine available out there; winemaking is more scientific than ever; and annual wine production regularly outpaces consumption. And yet your favorite wine keeps going in price! The solution is to enjoy "the next big thing" before it becomes "THE big thing." Rest assured that for every wine that gets too big for its britches, there is an underappreciated treasure produced somewhere else in the wine world that will make you just as happy.

Part 3

The Wine Universe

Chapter 7

The Region-Versus-Variety Debate

AS YOU STROLL THROUGH your favorite wine store, you'll notice that some wines are labeled by grape variety (such as Merlot and Chardonnay), while others are labeled with place names (such as Pomerol and Pouilly-Fuissé). Why is this so?

Old-World Distinctions

Perhaps because every inch of European soil has long been spoken for, European *vignerons* have historically placed primary importance on the geographic origin of wine rather than its grape variety. Long before quality wine was produced all over the world, the many centuries of trial and error had already helped wine producers in France, Italy, Germany, and elsewhere in Europe to match the best-suited *vinifera* grape variety with its proper venue. French winemakers found, for instance, that Cabernet Sauvignon could ripen beautifully in a warm, sunny autumn in the Médoc, while Pinot Noir ripened at its own ideal pace in the cooler, continental climate of Burgundy. In the Piedmont region of Northern Italy, the Nebbiolo grape became a superstar, one that refuses thus far to perform its magic on any other soil.

Yesterday's experiments have lead to today's wine laws, and so most European wine laws now dictate the grape varieties allowed for each region. Thus, when you buy a European bottle, it is usually—although not always—labeled primarily by its geographic origin, and the grape varieties used to make it are stipulated by law. Wine in the New World, however, is a different story.

New-World Differences

California was the first commercially successful outpost for European wine grapes in the New World. In the 1800s, the Golden State not only proved that it could produce high-quality wine occasionally on par with the finest wines of Europe, it also demonstrated a cost-effective capacity to produce inexpensive "jug wine" for the immigrant working class, for whom a glass or two of wine with a meal was no more special than coffee with breakfast. What better way to label such wine, it was thought at the time, than with familiar place-names from the old country? Thus, an ocean of Californian "rhine," "chianti," "hock," "burgundy," and "chablis" flowed forth to consumers across America, who were pleased to enjoy an inexpensive wine that was at least as good as the village wine back home.

However, this left the quality-oriented Californian producers in a quandary—place-names like "Calistoga" and "Napa" had little or no meaning to the wine connoisseur, yet co-opting a high-end place-name such as "Margaux" would be both unseemly and deceiving. The solution was to label by the grape variety used to make the wine, to better demonstrate that a "choice" variety—such as the Cabernet Sauvignon grape responsible for great wines of Bordeaux—was used in pure form to produce the wine. Thus, "varietal" labeling was born.

In contrast to the many centuries of trial and error that led to the development of European wine laws, there has been a relatively short period of experimentation in the New World. Wine producers in California, the Pacific Northwest, Australia, South America, and elsewhere are constantly planting new grape varieties in relatively young wine regions. Therefore, it would make little or no sense to label a red wine simply "Napa Valley," where a half-dozen different premium red varieties are cultivated.

The Current Lay of the Land

Walk into almost any wine store today and you will find wines sorted by both grape variety and geographic origin. There will most likely be a "French" section, perhaps further divided into "Rhône," "Burgundy," and "Bordeaux" subsections. The Californian wines will be in a separate section altogether, and the wines from Australia in still another part of the store. And yet, you will find wine made from the Syrah grape in all three areas—Hermitage from France, Shiraz from Australia, and varietal Syrah from California. Ditto for wines made from Chardonnay, Sauvignon Blanc, and many other grapes. This doesn't happen in the grocery store, where oranges from Florida and California are found side by side, rather than in opposite ends of the produce section. That's because an orange is an orange, and the difference between Californian and Floridian oranges is negligible compared to the difference between Californian oranges and the lemons grown in an adjacent grove. And so while your local wine merchant might find it expedient to arrange his store by geographical origin, it would probably be more useful for the wine consumer if the wine store (and the rest of the wine universe) were organized according to grape variety.

Today's wine drinker appears to be learning to love wine one grape at a time. Cabernet Sauvignon and Chardonnay, arguably the king and queen of Napa Valley grapes, were the favorites of Californian fans in the 1970s. Then Merlot became wildly popular after the release of scientific research suggesting that red wine offered healthful properties, which convinced many white wine drinkers to change colors. Now Syrah is the flavor of the day, and wine consumers are greeting the worldwide profusion of fine Syrah/Shiraz–based wines with considerable enthusiasm. Of course, all wines, Syrah, Merlot, or otherwise, have to come from somewhere. Yet, with few exceptions, the modern wine consumer is primarily buying wine according to the grape variety, not the region of origin.

Chapter 8

Varietal Wines, Grape by Grape

UNLESS LABELED OTHERWISE as "pear wine," "blueberry wine," or something else, it is safe to assume from the label on a bottle that "wine" is produced from grapes. There are many species of grapes, however, and grape varieties vary greatly in color and character, as well as in winemaking potential. Most of the world's wines come from the *Vitis vinifera* species, the classic European grape family whose vines were first brought to America prior to the American Revolution. Due to the *phylloxera* vine pest, however, the *vinifera* vines didn't produce much wine in the New World for more than a century. Instead, early American wine came from a variety of other grape species, including the East Coast's native *Vitis labrusca* grapes; the Ohio River Valley's *Vitis riparia* species; and the *Vitis rotundifolia* grape species. The Scuppernong grape of the American Southeast, thought to be the first native grape that American settlers tried to turn into wine, is a member of this last species.

Vitis labrusca's most famous family member is the Concord

grape. Although presently it is not given much serious consideration by the wine world, decent wine can be coaxed from it, as long as enough sugar is added to mitigate Concord's enamel-stripping acidity. Generally, these grapes are used to make grape juice and grape jelly rather than wine, although there is a century-old tradition of producing cloyingly sweet kosher wine from the Concord grape. Other *labrusca* grapes used more in the past than in American wine-making today are the Catawba, Delaware, and Niagara varieties. The biggest contribution that native North American grapes have made to the wine world is to provide rootstock for *vinifera* vines. As mentioned earlier in this book, many of the *vinifera* vines around the world today are grafted onto *Vitis riparia* vine roots, which are resistant to the destructive *phylloxera* vine louse.

The *vinifera* family of grapes, which come in red-, black-, and green-skinned varieties, is used to make the vast majority of the world's wine. There are hundreds of *vinifera* grape varieties, but only a few dozen of these—generally called "aromatic" varieties—are suitable for wine production. Of these, only a few are used to produce the world's finest wines. These "noble grape varieties" include Cabernet Sauvignon, Pinot Noir, Merlot, Syrah, Sangiovese, and Nebbiolo among the red wine grapes, as well as the white wine grapes Riesling, Chardonnay, and Sauvignon Blanc.

Varietal wines—those labeled and sold according to the grape variety from which they are made—must meet government-mandated minimum varietal percentages. In other words, there is a minimum percentage of a wine that must be made from the grape variety indicated on the label for it to be labeled as such. Although the label on your bottle may say Chardonnay, there is a very good chance that the wine is a blend made from Chardonnay and other grapes. However, these minor-percentage grapes are usually not credited on the bottle.

Varietal Correctness

A wine is described as "varietally correct" if the grape variety is easily discernable from the aroma and taste of the wine. Although wine made from a particular grape variety will also display traits associated with its geographical origin, there are certain qualities we have come to associate with the most common grape varieties no matter where they are produced.

Why are varietal wines so popular? Because the grape variety used to make the wine is the single most important determinant of the wine's flavor. The "aromatic" grape varieties are just that—they impart a recognizable set of aromas and flavors to wine.

Following is a breakdown of the most common and popular grape varieties.

Red Wine Grapes

Cabernet Sauvignon

Main growing regions: Bordeaux (France), Australia, California, Washington State, Chile, and Tuscany (Italy)
Aromas and flavors: Black currants, green peppers, chocolate, and mint
Acidity: Moderate
Tannin: Moderate to prominent
Body: Medium to full
Major mixing partners: Sangiovese (Tuscany), Merlot (Bordeaux), Shiraz (Australia)

Cabernet Sauvignon is perhaps the noblest red variety of all. Although its precise origins are unknown, Cabernet Sauvignon first became noteworthy as a grape variety in Bordeaux in the late 1700s. Today, this variety is at or near the top of every connoisseur's great red varietal list. Appearing either alone or in combination with other grape varieties, Cabernet Sauvignon generally makes rich, tannic wines capable of commanding high prices. The most expensive and well made of these often need a few years of aging in order to display their fine qualities fully—multiple layers of fruit flavors and a smooth but firm tannic structure. Cabernet Sauvignon benefits from contact with new oak, which lends balance and further complexity.

There are several exquisite versions of Cabernet Sauvignon from California, particularly the Napa Valley, that are not blended with other grapes. One of the most famous and expensive of these is Heitz Cellar "Martha's Vineyard" Cabernet Sauvignon. President Ronald Reagan proudly served the 1974 vintage of this wine to the president of France at a state dinner. Many top California wine producers have recently begun to combine Cabernet Sauvignon with other grapes that offer complementary flavors.

As a blending grape, Cabernet Sauvignon successfully shares a bottle with Syrah (Shiraz) in wines from Australia, and with Sangiovese in "super-Tuscan" wines from Italy. In Bordeaux, Cabernet Sauvignon is usually blended with a combination of Merlot, Cabernet Franc (one of its parent grapes), Malbec, and/or Petite Verdot. It is this Bordeaux blend that has found favor in California. As mentioned earlier, because United States law requires a minimum of 75 percent of a particular grape variety to qualify for varietal labeling, the California wine industry coined the term "Meritage," to distinguish these fine blended wines from ordinary table wines that similarly do not qualify for varietal labeling.

In any wine shop you might find varietal Cabernet Sauvignon from Chile, Australia, California, Washington State, Italy, Spain, or France. Expensive as great Cabernet Sauvignon can be, the bargains are out there. Look for varietal wines from the South of France (labeled "vin du pays d'oc," the "country wine" from the Languedoc) and also from Chile. The Cabernet/Shiraz blends from Australia are often excellent values as well.

The finest and most sought-after versions of Cabernet Sauvignon come from several different countries.

California: There are a handful of ultra-expensive, reserve Cabernet Sauvignons and Meritage wines from the Napa Valley, including the previously mentioned Heitz Cellar "Martha's Vineyard," Screaming Eagle, Caymus Special Select, Harlan Estate, Opus One, Niebaum-Coppola Rubicon, and Phelps "Insignia."

Australia: From Penfold's comes the noteworthy Cabernet Sauvignon Bin 707.

Italy: "Super-Tuscan" reds from coastal Tuscany include Antinori's "Solaia," a blend of 90 percent Cabernet Sauvignon and 10 percent Sangiovese.

Chile: Although not yet available, there is good reason to expect super-premium Cabernet Sauvignon from this region in the near future.

It is in the Bordeaux subregions of Médoc and Graves, however, where the world's most elegant, age-worthy, and expensive Cabernet Sauvignon–based wines are produced. Two of the top-rated Bordeaux châteaux, Château Mouton-Rothschild and Château Latour, rely on Cabernet Sauvignon for 70 percent of their blends. These and other

Suggested Food Pairings

The assertive flavors of Cabernet Sauvignon—young or old—match nicely with lamb, beef, and other red meat dishes. Young Cabernet Sauvignon is especially well paired with meats from the grill because the youthful fruit flavors are a perfect counterpoint to the pleasantly bitter scorch imparted by the open fire.

highly rated Bordeaux châteaux produce wines that can age well for many decades and command hundreds of dollars for a bottle from a great year.

Recommended Cabernet Sauvignon

Name	Region	Price
Concha y Toro "Xplorador"	Maipo Valley, Chile	$7
Niebaum-Coppola Claret	California	$15
J. Lohr "Seven Oaks"	Paso Robles, CA	$16
Viña Montes "Alpha"	Curico Valley, Chile	$20
Château St. Jean	Sonoma, CA	$27
Woodward Canyon "Artist Series"	Columbia Valley, Washington	$40
Château Lynch-Bages 1998	Pauillac, Bordeaux	$75
Pine Ridge "Stag's Leap"	Napa Valley, CA	$80
Ornellaia 1999	Bolgheri, Tuscany, Italy	$150
Château Mouton-Rothschild 1998	Pauillac, Bordeaux	$250

Pinot Noir

Main growing regions: Burgundy (France), California, and
Oregon
Aromas and flavors: Cherries, raspberries, soil, cola, and
smoke
Acidity: Moderate to high
Tannin: Low to moderate
Body: Light to medium
Major mixing partners: None

If it were not so difficult to grow, Pinot Noir would enjoy a reputation for greatness equal to that of Cabernet Sauvignon. It is the noble
red grape of France's Burgundy region where, under ideal conditions,
it yields ruby-colored wines with a velvety richness that has seduced
wine lovers for centuries. Whereas the outstanding Cabernet Sauvignons of Bordeaux are predictably excellent without generating a lot
of unexpected emotion, great Pinot Noirs of Burgundy overwhelm
your senses every time with their striking beauty.

Unlike Cabernet Sauvignon, which traveled with ease from Bordeaux to California's warmer valleys, where it thrives in sunshine,
Pinot Noir has a harder time in this region. With the exception of a
few pockets (such as Santa Barbara, Sonoma Coast, and Carneros),
Pinot Noir ripens too quickly on the hot California valley floors and
tends to be flat and uninteresting. Pinot Noir seems to be more at
home up north in Oregon, however, where the long, cool growing
season allows the Pinot Noir fruit flavors to develop slowly.

Perhaps the best use of Pinot Noir grapes in California is as the
main component in brut rosé-style, Blanc de Noirs sparkling wines.
Several of the great French Champagne houses, in order to meet

growing worldwide demand, opened shop in California. Here they found that Pinot Noir, a vital component of Champagne in France, grows to greater ripeness in the California sunshine. More ripeness means more color in the skin, and more fruit flavors as well. When gently pressed and quickly removed from the vat, Pinot Noir skins lend a delightful "blush" of copper color to Champagne-method sparkling wine. In France, such ripeness is quite rare, and brut rosés from the Champagne region are accordingly uncommon and expensive. The better California versions are often an excellent value.

Decent Pinot Noir is never cheap. A good way to get to know this grape is by trying varietal-labeled Pinot Noir from the big, reputable Burgundy (Bourgogne as it's known in France) houses. These will usually be labeled "Bourgogne Pinot Noir." If you feel like paying

Suggested Food Pairings

Less pigmented than most red wine grapes, Pinot Noir wines usually have a brick-orange cast rather than a deep purple color. At its best, Pinot Noir is low in tannin and high in glycerine (hence, the "velvet"), with a lively, acidic backbone that gives length and focus to its typical flavors. Such structure makes Pinot Noir a highly versatile food wine.

Full-bodied red Burgundy from the Côte de Nuits subregion is made entirely from Pinot Noir and is a classic accompaniment to beef roasts. The lighter red Burgundies from the Côte de Beaune are perfect with game birds such as pheasant and partridge and can even pair well with fish dishes. The Pinot Noirs from Oregon can be very Burgundian in structure and range from a light Côte de Beaune style to a richer Côte de Nuits style; they match with food accordingly. The light, clean acidity and modest tannin of typical Pinot Noir makes it suitable with all but the lightest of seafood dishes.

for it, move up-market from there to the better red Burgundies, although this region is very difficult (and expensive) to get to know. The Chalonnais subregion of Burgundy offers two inexpensive and enjoyable Pinot Noir–based wines: Givry and Mercurey.

Many Oregonian interpretations of Pinot Noir are closer in style to their Burgundian brethren than they are to their Californian neighbors. Ask a reliable wine merchant to suggest a varietally correct (yet affordable) Pinot Noir.

Recommended Pinot Noir

Name	Region	Price
Antonin Rodet "Vieilles Vignes"	Chalonnaise, Burgundy, France	$12
Ramsay	North Coast, CA	$15
La Fusina Pinot Nero Langhe Rosso	Dogliani, Piedmont, Italy	$22
Cameron	Dundee, OR	$23
Daniel Rion, Nuits-St.-Georges "Les Grandes Vignes"	Burgundy, France	$42
Siduri "Pisoni Vineyard"	Santa Lucia Highlands, CA	$50
Domaine Drouhin "Cuvee Laurene"	Oregon	$50
Bitouzet-Prieur Volnay "Caillerets" 1999	Burgundy, France	$55
Domaine Comte Armand, Pommard "Clos Epeneaux" 1999	Burgundy, France	$100
Domaine Leroy, Clos de Vougeot 2000	Burgundy, France	$700

Merlot

Main growing regions: Bordeaux (France), California, Washington State, Australia, Chile, and Long Island

Aromas and flavors: Plums, currants, blackberries, mocha, and black cherries

Acidity: Low to moderate

Tannin: Low to moderate
Body: Medium
Major mixing partner: Cabernet Sauvignon (Bordeaux)

It is difficult to discuss Merlot without mentioning Cabernet Sauvignon. Just as Cabernet Sauvignon gained recognition in the Médoc subregion of Bordeaux in the late 1700s, so too did Merlot become prominent in the Bordeaux subregions of Pomerol and Saint-Emilion. These two subregions are cooler and wetter than the Médoc, but Merlot can ripen beautifully in these and other climates too cool for Cabernet Sauvignon. The infant wine region on the North Fork of Long Island, for instance, while not quite hot enough for quality Cabernet Sauvignon, shows great promise for Merlot.

Merlot is a distant relative of Cabernet Sauvignon. The biggest difference is that the skin of the Merlot grape is thinner than that of Cabernet Sauvignon; therefore, Merlot is the earlier ripening and less tannic of the two. Merlot has a reputation for making soft, round, and drinkable wines with low acidity and early maturity; yet, according to many experts just a few short years ago, Merlot had no future as a varietal wine in California. In the past few years, however, the Merlot grape has made the transition from being an assistant to Cabernet Sauvignon in blended wines to being a star in its own right. Consequently, it has become a somewhat overrated and misunderstood variety. How did this happen?

When the word got out from the medical journals that red wine was good for your heart, the resulting boom in red-wine sales just about equaled the sales of Beatles records after the rumors of Paul McCartney's death circulated. The wine-drinking public, already hooked on white Zinfandel and Chardonnay, switched *en masse* to red wine. Nonwine drinkers, perhaps mindful of an unpleasant experience

Suggested Food Pairings

The soft tannin in Merlot also makes it an enjoyable match with a broad variety of foods. Even seafood, especially from the grill, makes a successful pairing with Merlot's unobtrusive flavors. Its somewhat bland personality also allows Merlot to fit nicely with all types of well-seasoned ethnic dishes.

with dry, tannic, red wine, wanted a supple, drinkable red wine. These consumers turned to Merlot, because of its reputation for low acid and its softness.

California was unprepared for this market shift, with only a few new acres of this variety planted since the mid-1970s. It seems that every winery that was able planted additional Merlot acreage as soon as possible, and the resulting wines were often disappointing. Too often, people buy a Merlot that is shaped more by market forces than by the winemaker's art. These sorts of wines are made out of grapes from very young vines grown at crop levels far too high for fine wine production. It is quite a challenge to find delicious, varietally correct Merlot for under $8.

That being said, there are a few sources of bargains in varietal Merlot. French Merlots labeled "vin de pays d'oc" are often excellent values, and there are many versions of Merlot available for under $10. South America (Chile and Argentina) produces good, affordable Merlot as well.

What are the characteristics of a good Merlot? Look for rich, plum-like fruit, almost jammy in its concentration, and low levels of acid and tannin. Merlot does not get particularly complex; yet because of its soft tannin and gentle acidity profile, its pleasing fruit flavors are more accessible than those in sturdier reds.

Recommended Merlot

Name	Region	Price
Domaine des Fontanelles	Vin de Pays d'Oc, France	$7
Columbia Crest "Grand Estates"	Columbia Valley, WA	$11
Blackstone	California	$12
Falesco	Umbria, Italy	$18
Casa Lapostolle "Cuvée Alexandre"	Rapel Valley, Chile	$19
Nelson Estate	Sonoma, CA	$20
Raphael	North Fork of Long Island, NY	$35
L'Ecole No. 41	Walla Walla Valley, WA	$40
Beringer "Howell Mountain—Bancroft Ranch"	Napa Valley, CA	$80
Château Le Bon-Pasteur	Pomerol, Bordeaux	$80

Syrah/Shiraz

Main growing regions: Rhône (France), Australia, and California

Aromas and flavors: Plums, spices, blackberries, and blueberries

Acidity: low to moderate

Tannin: Moderate to prominent

Body: Medium

Major mixing partners: Grenache and Mourvedre (Rhône and Languedoc) and Cabernet Sauvignon (Australia)

The Syrah grape, known as Shiraz in Australia and South Africa, is a noble grape variety held in high esteem by many red-wine lovers. The great and ageworthy wines of the northern Rhône—Hermitage, Côte

Rôtie, St. Joseph, and Cornas—are produced from Syrah. For many years the finest wine produced in Australia has been Penfold's Grange, and there are of late a handful of other Australian Shiraz–based wines competing for the honor. Australian varietal Shiraz—as well as Shiraz blended with Cabernet Sauvignon—are often remarkable bargains.

California got a late start with this variety. It seems that another grape from the Rhône valley, perhaps the Duriff grape, was transplanted by accident instead of Syrah. Today, that grape is known in California as Petite Sirah, and the true Syrah is a relatively recent arrival in California. Some California Syrahs are quite good, but Australia, with a 100-year head start, remains the better source for bargains in Shiraz.

In general, the French version is higher in acid and better with food than the Australian version, which shows more fruit. This is because of the difference in climate. The warmer weather of Australia leads to a more thorough ripening of the grape, which in turn leads to more fruitiness and a lower acidity in the wine. Whereas the French Syrahs tend to display raspberry-like fruit aromas, the Australian versions are often more suggestive of raisins.

Syrah is, in some ways, the "Next Big Grape." Wine made from Syrah is often a middleweight like Merlot, not heavy like a big, tannic

Suggested Food Pairings

Many versions of Syrah have a whiff of spiciness, and this dimension of flavor suggests a pairing with exotic seasonings, such as those found in many Asian cuisines.

Cabernet Sauvignon, and it grows beautifully in all of the most important wine regions in the world.

Petite Sirah, genetically unrelated to the true Syrah, has found a happy home in sunny and hot California. Like Zinfandel, Petite Sirah vines often live to be 100 years old, and "old-vine" versions of Petite Sirah can be beautifully dense, rich, and velvety.

Recommended Syrah/Shiraz

Name	Region	Price
Cline	California	$10
Woop Woop	Australia	$12
Saint Cosme Côtes-du-Rhône	Rhône, France	$12
Jade Mountain	Napa Valley, CA	$25
Errazuriz Reserva	Aconcagua Valley, Chile	$27
Columbia Winery "Red Willow Vineyard"	Woodinville, WA	$35
Isole Olena IGT	Tuscany, Italy	$42
Rosemount "Balmoral"	McLaren Vale, South Australia	$50
Guigal Hermitage 2000	Rhône, France	$60
Penfold's Grange 1998	South Australia	$200

Recommended Petite Sirah

Name	Region	Price
Bogle	California	$10
Foppiano, Paso Robles	Paso Robles, CA	$18
Lolonis "Orpheus"	Redwood Valley, Mendocino, CA	$28
Stag's Leap Vineyard	Stag's Leap, Napa Valley, CA	$33

Zinfandel

Main growing region: California
Aromas and flavors: Blackberry jam and black pepper
Acidity: Low to moderate
Tannin: Moderate; can be substantial in some versions, light in others
Body: Medium to full
Major mixing partners: Often blended, but rarely credited (California)

This popular grape of unclear origin (recent DNA analysis suggests Eastern Europe) showed up in California in the mid-1800s and has been growing like a weed since then. No other *vinifera* grape thrives as well on Californian heat and sunshine. Unfortunately, the evolution of Zinfandel got sidetracked by the creation of the wildly popular rosé, white Zinfandel, the inspiration for which evolved during a period of slack demand for red wine in the early 1970s.

As a result of this, wine lists must now use the retronym "Red Zinfandel" to indicate the varietal in its original form. Zinfandel is as versatile as it is prolific, capable of a broad range of styles. In addition to White Zinfandel, which is actually a rosé, Zinfandel can range from a light, Beaujolais-like quaff to late-harvest brutes that practically ooze pepper and jammy fruit. Although $5 won't get you a bottle of Zinfandel, $10 bottles do exist, and they are often quite good.

If you suffer sticker shock from a reserve Cabernet Sauvignon or Meritage, opt for an estate-bottled "old vines" Zinfandel ($20 to $30). Its complexity, power, and balance should impress you for the money.

White Zinfandel was wildly popular for a few years after it first reached the market in the early 1970s, and it is still the wine of choice for people who otherwise would not drink wine. The noticeable residual sugar (around 1.5 percent), lower alcohol content (10 percent or so), and fresh strawberry fruit flavor give White Zinfandel its broad appeal.

Contrary to what many wine snobs would have you believe, there are several White Zinfandels of quality on the market. The key to good White Zinfandel lies in the color. While many of the palest pink versions are rather bland, the darker versions tend to have more fruit flavors.

Suggested Food Pairings

Zinfandel wines are especially well matched with roasted lamb, other Mediterranean dishes, and even hearty vegetable dishes. Zinfandel stands up well to garlic and powerful seasonings. These buxom, fruity wines are great in a variety of situations, whether alone or with a wine-friendly snack of cheese and crackers.

When it comes to White Zinfandel, there is one particular "match made in heaven" worth noting: White Zinfandel with Thanksgiving dinner. An American holiday deserves an American wine, and the fruitiness and residual sugar of White Zinfandel helps to wash down even the most dried-out turkey breast. Also, because Thanksgiving dinner—turkey and root vegetables, usually—is relatively inexpensive to prepare, White Zinfandel represents an intelligent price matching. Finally, if you celebrate this annual feast with elderly relatives who are not wine buffs, they will probably find White Zinfandel more enjoyable than any other wine.

Recommended Zinfandel/Primitivo

Name	Region	Price
A Mano Primitivo	Apulia, Italy	$10
Ravenswood "Vintner's Blend"	California	$11
Easton, Amador County	Amador, CA	$14
Sausal "Family"	Alexander Valley, Sonoma, CA	$15
Edmeades	Mendocino, CA	$17
Rabbit Ridge "Westside"	Paso Robles, CA	$17
Dashe Cellars, Dry Creek	Dry Creek, Sonoma, CA	$23
Howell Mountain Vineyards "Old Vines"	Howell Mountain, Napa Valley, CA	$35

Nebbiolo

Main growing regions: Piedmont (Italy)

Aromas and flavors: Raspberries, mushrooms, plums, leather, and earth

Acidity: Relatively high

Tannin: Prominent in youth, "dusty" with age

Body: Medium

Major mixing partners: None (Some minor, local grapes are blended with Nebbiolo in certain Piedmont wines.)

Named for the dense fogs so prevalent in the vineyards of Piedmont, Italy, the Nebbiolo grape is responsible for several of Italy's—and the world's—finest red wines. The great red wines of Piedmont—Barolo, Barbaresco, Ghemme, Gattinara—are regarded by aficionados as members of the exclusive club of the greatest wines in the world. Nebbiolo grapes have not as yet done well when grown away from their native soil, but somewhere outside of Italy, perhaps, there is a piece of land just waiting to be converted into a great Nebbiolo vineyard. Some growers in California have begun experimenting with Nebbiolo, but they have met with limited success so far.

In the past, the best of these wines, like many Cabernet Sauvignons, were too tannic to drink in their youth and required a decade or so of cellaring. Perhaps more than any other grape variety, Nebbiolo rewards patience. However, more Nebbiolo-based wines are being vinified to be enjoyable in their youth. If you're looking for an affordable way to get to know Nebbiolo, try a Nebbiolo d'Alba or other varietal Nebbiolo from Piedmont selected by a wine merchant or reviewer you trust. Entry level for these wines is $20 or more. If you see one of these wines from a great year such as 1997 or 2000, it might be a bargain, even if it is a little out of your normal price range.

Because Nebbiolo has not been transplanted with widespread success from its native Piedmont, it is difficult to differentiate between the characteristics of the grape and those of the region. Look for Piedmont Nebbiolos to be very dry, flavorful but not heavy on the

Suggested Food Pairings

Despite their powerful flavors, Barolo and other Nebbiolo-based Italian wines need to be served with food since they are considerably more acidic than equally serious New-World wines. Because the Nebbiolo grape doesn't travel as of yet, it is difficult to abstract out its varietal character from the character of the Piedmontese *terroir*. No matter—we can still pair food with Nebbiolo without really knowing if we are matching food to the region or the grape. The Italian Nebbiolos are a natural match with rich, earthy dishes such as game and red meat with mushrooms. Even chicken, if prepared in a rustic manner, can hold its own with most of these wines.

palate, and surprisingly subtle and complex. Watch for the California version, which should become more prevalent in the years ahead, to have stronger plum and raspberry fruit flavors than those from Italy.

Recommended Nebbiolo

Name	Region	Price
Aurelio Settimo, Langhe Nebbiolo DOC 2000	Piedmont, Italy	$18
Produttori del Barbaresco, Barbaresco "Torre" 1998	Piedmont, Italy	$28
Elio Grasso, Barolo "Ginestra Casa Mate" 1998	Piedmont, Italy	$45
Marchesi di Gresy, Barbaresco "Camp Gros" 1998	Piedmont, Italy	$79
Giacomo Conterno, Barolo "Cascina Francia" 1998	Piedmont, Italy	$100
Roberto Voerzio, Barolo "Brunate" 1999	Piedmont, Italy	$200

Sangiovese

Main growing regions: Tuscany (Italy), some California

Aromas and flavors: Cherries, raisins, earth, leather, and violets

Acidity: Moderate to high

Tannin: Light to moderate

Body: Light to medium

Major mixing partners: Cabernet Sauvignon (Italy) and Cannaiolo Nero (Italy)

Sangiovese is an Italian grape that, like the Nebbiolo, hasn't made a significant impact on the wine world when grown outside of Italy. It is the most important grape variety in central Italy, especially in Tuscany. In this region, the surprisingly sophisticated Etruscans made delicious wine well before the rise of the Roman Empire. The Sangiovese grape tends to generate closely related mutations. In fact, the

Brunello and Sangiovetto grapes are such close relatives of Sangiovese that they are usually considered to be Sangiovese itself.

It might be said that, in terms of style, Sangiovese is to Nebbiolo what Pinot Noir is to Cabernet Sauvignon. Like an excellent Burgundy, many great Sangiovese wines, while ageworthy, can also be quite enjoyable before their fifth birthday.

Like other noble grape varieties, Sangiovese can be a prince or a pauper, and the pauper, a varietal-labeled Sangiovese from one of Italy's many regions, is frequently a bargain. Early attempts at this varietal in California tend to cost like the prince but taste like the pauper. So far, California winemakers have had a difficult time getting Sangiovese acclimated to the warmth and sunshine of their vineyards. However, a few producers have produced some good Sangioveses, albeit at Sauvignon-like prices.

Varietally labeled Sangiovese can be surprisingly inexpensive. Look for the typical cherry fruit, high acid, low tannin, and glycerine.

In the Chianti region, the Sangiovese grape has historically been blended with the local Cannaiolo grape as well as two white grapes: Trebbiano and Malvasia. Presently, the top producers are omitting the white grapes, in favor of more Sangiovese.

Suggested Food Pairings

Because of its combination of characteristics, Sangiovese has few equals as a red wine to accompany seafood. When matching food and wine, remember also to match price along with other characteristics. In this sense, inexpensive, varietally labeled Sangiovese is a good pizza and spaghetti wine. These wines are usually better than those inexpensive, silly-looking, straw-covered bottles of cheap Chianti you used to see at Italian restaurants.

Suggested Food Pairings

The great Chianti Classico and Brunello di Montalcino wines go well with veal, beef, lamb, and hearty chicken dishes. Sangiovese-based wines also stand up well with tomato sauce. Super-Tuscans, with their sturdy framework of Cabernet Sauvignon, are generally best reserved for red meat and game.

The "super-Tuscan" red wines that first came to our market in the early 1980s are a blend of Sangiovese and Cabernet Sauvignon. These superior wines lie outside of Italy's wine classification system, but they are more intensely flavored than Chianti and are worth a try if you are looking to splurge.

Recommended Sangiovese

Name	Region	Price
Gini, Chianti DOC *straw bottle*	Tuscany, Italy	$9
La Carraia, Sangiovese IGT	Umbria, Italy	$12
Poliziano, Rosso di Montepulciano 2002	Tuscany, Italy	$15
Fattoria le Pupille, Morellino di Scansano 2002	Tuscany, Italy	$15
Long Vineyards "Seghesio Vineyards"	Sonoma, CA	$23
Poliziano, Vino Nobile di Montepulciano 2000	Tuscany, Italy	$25
Altesino, Rosso di Montalcino 2002	Tuscany, Italy	$30
Altesino, Brunello di Montalcino 1998	Tuscany, Italy	$60
Antinori "Tignanello" 2000	Tuscany, Italy	$75
Castello di Ama, Chianti Classico DOCG "Casuccia" 1997	Tuscany, Italy	$190

Grenache

Main growing regions: Spain, Rhône (France), and California
Aroma and flavor: Raspberry
Acidity: Moderate
Body: Medium to full
Major mixing partners: Syrah (France) and Tempranillo
(Spain)

The Southern Rhône valley of France is famous for its sturdy, drinkable, and affordable red wines. Many different grape varieties are grown here, but Grenache is the predominant variety and is the primary grape among the many used to make Côtes-du-Rhône rouge. This popular wine has ample body, meaty structure, and a straightforward fruit flavor of raspberry jam. Côtes-du-Rhône is a genuine bargain among French red wines, usually retailing for less than $10 per bottle. The dry rosés of the neighboring Southern French regions are also made primarily from the Grenache grape and are considered by many experts to be the finest pink wines in the world.

Suggested Food Pairings

Well-made Grenache-based wines tend to have enough body and character to be enjoyable with or without food. Hearty beef and lamb dishes, especially stews made with Côtes-du-Rhône as an ingredient, seem to bring out the delightful spiciness in Grenache. The most powerful versions of Châteauneuf-du-Pape stand up well to steak au poivre and other powerfully seasoned dishes, whereas tamer bottlings match well with goose, duck, and the like—not summer food, and not summer wine. In hot weather, try pairing a French Tavel or a California rosé with a salad or simple picnic fare.

Under the local name Garnacha, Grenache is extensively planted in Spain and Portugal. It lends some fruit to the relatively austere Tempranillo grape in the red wines of Rioja (Spain). In California it is vinified in bulk for use in rosés and red jug wines, although some wineries are experimenting with upscale rosés. California Grenache varietal wines, although somewhat scarce, can be quite good.

To experience Grenache in its purest state, look for Château Rayas from Châteauneuf-du-Pape. Although AOC law allows the use of as many as thirteen different grapes for Châteauneuf-du-Pape red, most of these wines are predominantly Grenache, and Château Rayas eschews all other permitted varieties to make a 100-percent Grenache wine. This costs more than $100 per bottle, though.

Recommended Grenache/Garnacha

Name	Region	Price
Principe de Viana, Agramont "Old Vines" Garnacha	Navarra, Spain	$6
Guigal Côtes-du-Rhône	Rhône, France	$11
Bonny Doon "Clos de Gilroy"	California	$13
Domaine Montirius Gigondas	Rhône, France	$25
Domaine de la Janasse Châteauneuf-du-Pape	Rhône, France	$35
Alban "Estate Vineyard"	Edna Valley, CA	$45

Gamay

Main growing region: Beaujolais (France)
Aromas and flavors: Strawberries and raspberries
Acidity: Moderate
Tannin: Low
Body: Light
Major mixing partners: None

The granite soil of the Beaujolais, the southernmost subregion of Burgundy, brings out the best qualities of the Gamay grape. The red wine of Beaujolais is fresh, light, and fruity, and it is enjoyed all over the world. The lively fruit flavors—strawberry and raspberry—show well in the absence of substantial tannin. These qualities lend themselves well to carbonic maceration (whole berry fermentation in the complete absence of oxygen). This process protects the delicate fruit components and readies the wine for early release.

Beaujolais Nouveau, the first release of red Beaujolais, reaches the market the third Thursday in November, immediately following the harvest. It is eagerly awaited by the wine world as the first indication of the quality of the entire vintage, so a delicious Beaujolais Nouveau is cause for rejoicing among the French.

The Gamay grape reaches its summit of quality in the "*cru* Beaujolais" wines. These are red wines produced from Gamay grapes grown within the ten townships regarded as superior to the rest of the subregion: Moulin-à-Vent, Brouilly, Côte de Brouilly, Fleurie, Chiroubles, Morgon, Chénas, Juliénas, St-Amour, and Régnié. Taken together, these townships comprise the heart of the Beaujolais subregion. It has been observed that these wines, unlike other wines from Beaujolais, can benefit from a few years of aging.

California does produce, albeit sparingly, two wines whose names imply Gamay—Napa Gamay and Gamay Beaujolais. Napa Gamay is actually the lowly Gros Auxerrois grape from Southwest France, and Gamay Beaujolais is an inferior mutation of Pinot Noir. For price and quality, stick to the French version, especially during the Nouveau season when California "Gamay Nouveau" labels are intentionally deceiving and the wines are decidedly inferior to the real thing.

The Georges Duboeuf firm is the king of Beaujolais wine producers. The quality and pricing of its wines are more than fair. Louis

Suggested Food Pairings

With its pleasant balance of fruit over tannin, a Gamay-based wine can take a slight chilling and may be offered with just about any food, from poached salmon to barbecued pork ribs. These wines, with their overt fruitiness, are also enjoyable alone.

Jadot is another reliable bottler of Beaujolais. These two firms bottle the full spectrum of wine from this subregion: Beaujolais Nouveau, Beaujolais-Villages, and all of the *crus*.

Recommended Gamay

Name	Region	Price
Georges Duboeuf, Beaujolais-Villages	Beaujolais, Burgundy, France	$7
Domaine des Braves, Regnie	Beaujolais, Burgundy, France	$13
Louis Jadot, Moulin-à-Vent "Château des Jacques"	Beaujolais, Burgundy, France	$20

Tempranillo

Main growing region: Rioja (Spain)
Aromas and flavors: Not very fruity; leather, spice, cherries, and raisins
Acidity: Low to moderate
Tannin: Low to moderate
Body: Medium
Major mixing partner: Grenache/Garnacha (Rioja)

You rarely see Tempranillo bottled as a varietal, but it is included here because of the importance of Rioja, an affordable treasure from

Suggested Food Pairings

As a light- to medium-bodied red with modest acidity, red Rioja matches well with grilled fish, generously seasoned vegetable dishes, and pasta. It also pairs well with chicken and red meats. As such, Rioja might accurately be called a fool-proof red wine.

Spain. Tempranillo-based Rioja-region wines range from very inexpensive but enjoyable varieties to fabulously expensive, world-class versions. The inexpensive versions often display the body of Pinot Noir without the flashy fruit. The subtle cherry fruit of Tempranillo is often well masked by smoky flavors and oakiness. Grenache (Garnacha) is the minority blending partner in Rioja, and it adds some fruitiness to the wine. The greatest versions of Rioja cost as much as any great wine and show a depth and length of flavors that justify their price.

The Tempranillo-based Rioja wines are a great value, and they are easy to appreciate. Rioja is a good place for the neophyte to start in his or her exploration of red wine.

Recommended Tempranillo/Tinto Fino

Name	Region	Price
Bodegas Bretón "Loriñon" Tinto	Rioja Alta	$12
Clos du Bois	Alexander Valley, Sonoma, CA	$16
Bodegas Montecillo, Rioja Gran Reserva	Rioja	$25
Teófilo Reyes	Ribero del Duero	$28
Truchard	Napa Valley, CA	$32
Pesquera Reserva	Ribero del Duero	$45

Malbec

Main growing regions: Bordeaux and Cahors (France),
   Argentina
Aromas and flavors: Raspberry, chocolate, and spice
Acidity: Can be low or moderately high depending on origin
Body: Medium to full
Major mixing partner: Other Bordeaux varieties

Malbec ripens early, usually a week or so after the Merlot is harvested. Malbec is a relatively minor Bordeaux variety, but it has managed to attain stardom on its own. Malbec is often the primary grape variety in the Côtes de Blaye subregion of Bordeaux, which is situated across the Gironde River from the Médoc. Although it is used less and less in Bordeaux, Malbec is the main grape in the wines of Cahors, in Southwestern France. Malbec has not caught on especially well in California, where it is used sparingly in "Meritage" wines.

Argentina, however, is another story. A century ago, the Malbec grape was brought to Argentina, where it thrives in the hot, dry summers of these eastern foothills of the Andes. Malbec may well be considered the national grape of Argentina, and there are many quality versions on the market for less than $10. Argentinean producers have been focusing more and more on quality in the past decade, and some increasingly pricey—and exquisite—Argentine Malbecs have been

Suggested Food Pairings

The Argentines enjoy their Malbecs with their famously grass-fed beef. The growing movement toward naturally raised, grass-fed beef provides us with an easy match with full-bodied Argentine Malbec.

reaching our shelves and scoring well with the wine critics. Don't be too shocked to see $50 versions in your wine shop . . . dollar for dollar, these Malbecs compete favorably with Californian Cabernet Sauvignons.

Recommended Malbec

Name	Region	Price
Gascon	Argentina	$10
Château du Cedre 2000	Cahors, France	$11
Ricardo Santos	Argentina	$16
Château Roland La Garde 2000	Côtes de Blaye, Bordeaux	$30
Catena "Alta"	Argentina	$50

Cabernet Franc

Main growing regions: Bordeaux and Loire (France), California, Northeastern U.S.

Aromas and flavors: Cherries, pencil lead, dust, currants, and herbs

Acidity: Moderate

Body: Light

Major mixing partner: Other Bordeaux varieties

Cabernet Franc, "the other Cabernet," in Bordeaux, is more commonly used in blends than as a stand-alone varietal wine. Recent DNA analysis suggests that Cabernet Franc is a parent grape of Cabernet Sauvignon. Although Cabernet Franc grapes require ample heat accumulation in order to ripen fully, the Cabernet Franc vine is perhaps the hardiest of all *vinifera* vines and is able to withstand a harshly cold winter. For this reason alone there is considerable acreage of Cabernet Franc growing in the northeastern United States. However, it appears that few northeastern vineyards other than those on the especially warm north fork of Long Island can bring this grape to full ripeness.

There are several excellent Californian versions of Cabernet Franc, although they are overshadowed by the more popular Cabernet Sauvignons. Cabernet Franc is a star in France's Loire Valley, where it is made into a light and agreeable red in the appellations Chinon and Bourgueil. In Bordeaux, the earlier-ripening Cabernet Franc offers a safety net to Médoc *vignerons* whose later-ripening Cabernet Sauvignon may be damaged by autumn rains. Across the Dordogne river, Cabernet Franc is an important blending partner to Merlot in the St. Emilion district.

Recommended Cabernet Franc

Name	Region	Price
Ironstone	California	$10
Domaine Joguet Chinon	Loire Valley, France	$16
Standing Stone	Finger Lakes, NY	$16
Pride Mountain Vineyards	Sonoma, CA	$50
Château Cheval Blanc 1998	St. Emilion, Bordeaux	$400

Barbera

Main growing regions: Piedmont, Lombardy (Italy); the Central Valley of California

Aromas and flavors: Indistinct aromas, strong "grapey" flavors

Acidity: Moderate to rapier-like

Tannin: Light

Body: Medium
Major mixing partners: Barbera sneaks into some Nebbiolo-based Piedmont wines; also blended with Zinfandel for "jug" wine in California

While the Nebbiolo is Piedmont's royal grape, Barbera is perhaps the region's most useful. Ripening after the Dolcetto but before the Nebbiolo, Barbera makes a hearty, powerful wine whose prominent acidity makes it compatible with assertively flavored Piedmontese dishes. In California the Barbera grape is relegated to workhorse status. Like the white Chenin Blanc, Barbera maintains its high acidity at high crop levels and in the blistering heat of California's vast San Joaquin Valley.

Recommended Barbera

Name	Region	Price
Martilde, Barbera Oltrepo Pavese DOC	Lombardy, Italy	$13
Cantina del Pino, Barbera d'Alba DOC	Piedmont, Italy	$17
Coppo "Camp du Rouss" Barbera d'Asti DOC	Piedmont, Italy	$19
Renwood	Amador, CA	$20

Suggested Food Pairings

Barbera is a perfect pasta and pizza red that pairs especially well with tomato-based sauces.

White Wine Grapes

Chardonnay

Main growing regions: Burgundy (France), California,
    Oregon, Washington State, Australia, New Zealand, South
    Africa, and Chile
Aromas and flavors: Varies greatly by region: vanilla, tropical
    fruits, toast, and nuts
Acidity: Moderate to high
Body: Light to moderate
Major mixing partner: Semillon (Australia)

The wine-drinking public is so accustomed to saying, "I'll have a Chardonnay," it's worth reminding that Chardonnay is the name of a white-wine grape variety. In fact, Chardonnay is the most popular and most versatile white grape in the world, though it is not the most widely planted one. (That distinction belongs to Spain's Airén grape.)

Chardonnay grapes are used to make the austere, bone-dry wines of France's Chablis subregion, as well as the tropically fruity, almost syrupy white wines of California and Australia. It is also a crucial component of Champagne and the sole grape in the premium Champagne labeled "Blanc de Blancs." Chardonnay is responsible for the great white Burgundies from France—the most expensive dry white wines in the world. Finally, Chardonnay can even accommodate a dose of noble rot and yield a gloriously rich and sweet dessert wine, as it does in Southeastern Austria and elsewhere.

What makes Chardonnay so versatile? Perhaps Chardonnay has little indigenous character of its own and instead displays the best characteristics of the soil and climate in which it is grown, like a lawyer who can argue any side of an issue. However, in all of its incarnations Chardonnay does display a propensity for both glycerine and acid, whose interplay results in the most velvety, sensually delightful texture of all white wines. So, under all its trappings, Chardonnay is mostly about texture, and that is what you should always look for, even in simple Chardonnays. Unlike the red-wine kingpin Cabernet Sauvignon, there are many high-quality Chardonnays to be found in the $8 to $10 price range.

So what does Chardonnay taste like? It depends on whom you ask. It is difficult to define a standard of varietal correctness when a grape variety has so many personalities. However, some generalizations about Chardonnay can be made.

The astringent flavor imparted by oak barrels marries well with Chardonnay in different regions. So well, in fact, that it can be difficult to separate the flavor of the grape and the flavor of the oak in your mind. If you want to taste a pure, unoaked Chardonnay, look for a Chablis from the producer Jean-Marc Brocard, another of the handful of Chablis producers who eschew the use of oak in their winemaking.

To the south of Chablis in France is the Burgundy subregion of Côte de Beaune, where Chardonnay grapes are transformed into the world's greatest Chardonnay wines. Corton-Charlemagne, Meursault, and the various Montrachet vineyards produce beautifully structured Chardonnays that are brilliant and clean, with acidity, mouth-filling body, and aromas of toast, nuts, butter, and a variety of subtle fruits. When ripened in the California sunshine, the fruit aroma becomes more apparent.

Napa Valley, the first California appellation to excel with Chardonnay, tends to produce high-glycerine, well-oaked versions with ample fruit—apple and pear intermingled with oak. Drive over

Suggested Food Pairings

Because Chardonnay has such a range of styles, you should consider the type of Chardonnay when trying to find the right wine for a particular meal. Chablis is the driest, most acidic interpretation, and belongs with seafood, especially shellfish and delicate white fish like Dover sole or wild halibut. The rounder white Burgundies from the Côte de Beaune are also seafood wines but can accompany meats such as chicken and veal. However, seafood doesn't match so well with fruitier Chardonnays such as those from California and Australia.

If you insist on a fruity Chardonnay with your fish, California cuisine comes into play. The flavorful ingredients used in California cuisine—generous additions of fresh herbs and various chili peppers, and wood grilling—can transform a delicate piece of fish into a jam session of loud flavors. In this case, a big wine is called for, and California Chardonnay is ideal. In fact, big Chardonnays like these can stand up to many dishes not normally paired with white wine—even grilled meats!

Finally, if you want to drink Chardonnay without food, the Australian versions, with their generous fruit and mild acidity, are an excellent choice.

the Mayacamas mountain range into Sonoma Valley and you will find a more tropical element in Chardonnay, usually pineapple. The Santa Barbara growing area, far south of Napa/Sonoma, tends to bottle an even riper Chardonnay. The fruit impression there is even more tropical, and the acidity profile is quite soft.

For yet more fruit flavor, you must go to Australia. The grape-growing climate in Australia is unique to wine-producing countries. The Hunter Valley in Southeastern Australia experiences intense sunshine. This would normally overripen wine grapes, but the ripening effect of the sun in this region is greatly tempered by cool breezes. This combination of plentiful sunlight and refreshing air brings grapes to a full ripeness slowly, so as to develop the most intense flavors imaginable in Chardonnay. Suggestions of pineapple, coconut, and bananas spring forth from this deep-golden wine. These wines used to lack the necessary acidity, but innovative winemaking techniques seem to have solved this problem.

Recommended Chardonnay

Name	Region	Price
Lindeman's Bin 65	Padthaway, Australia	$7
Maison Louis Latour "Grand Ardeche"	Vin de Pays des Coteaux l'Ardeche	$9
Château St. Jean	Sonoma, CA	$15
Brocard Chablis "Domaine Ste. Claire"	Chablis, Burgundy, France	$16
Hamilton Russell Vineyards "Estate"	Walker Bay, South Africa	$19
Kumeu River 2002	Kumeu, North Island, New Zealand	$29
Château St. Michelle "Cold Creek Vineyard"	Columbia Valley, WA	$30
Long Vineyards "Estate Grown"	Napa Valley, CA	$33
Leeuwin Estate "Art Series"	Margret River, Australia	$65
Domaine Louis Latour Corton-Charlemagne 2001	Burgundy, France	$70

Sauvignon Blanc

Main growing regions: Bordeaux (France), Loire (France), California, New Zealand, and South Africa

Aromas and flavors: Cut grass, herbs, melon, gooseberry, and grapefruit; cat-box, in extreme versions

Acidity: High
Body: Light to medium
Major mixing partner: Semillon (Bordeaux)

In comparison to Chardonnay, it might take a little more wine knowledge to appreciate a great Sauvignon Blanc. That is because the hallmark of quality Sauvignon Blanc—bright, crisp acidity—is not as sensually pleasing as the seductive texture of good Chardonnay. "Grassy" and "herbaceous" are common descriptions of Sauvignon Blanc's fruit components.

An alternative vinification style of Sauvignon Blanc yields a richer wine. "Fumé Blanc" is the name for a style created in California in the 1960s by Robert Mondavi. Styled after the legendary Pouilly-Fumé of the Loire region in France, Fumé Blanc has a richer, fuller style.

There are a few world-class wines made from Sauvignon Blanc that earn this variety its place beside the other white noble grapes, Riesling and Chardonnay. Château Haut-Brion Blanc of Graves is universally regarded as the finest of its type and an equal to the great

Suggested Food Pairings

The high acidity of Sauvignon Blanc makes for a great pairing with seafood—Sancerre from the Loire; Graves Blanc from Bordeaux; and varietal Sauvignon Blanc from California, South Africa, and even New Zealand are perfect with fish. Whereas the Sauvignon Blancs are excellent with seafood, the more substantial Fumé Blanc can be paired with a wider variety of dishes, including chicken, veal, and pasta. Try serving a good Sauvignon Blanc with an uncomplicated seafood dish without telling your guests what they are drinking, and you will seem quite wine savvy once they figure it out.

white Burgundies. Close on its heels is Domaine de Chevalier, also from Graves. Sauvignon Blanc is blended with a lesser amount of Semillon in most Graves whites. This formula is reversed in the dessert wines from neighboring Sauternes.

In spite of its legitimate claim to nobility, Sauvignon Blanc might well have an inferiority complex. The public hasn't taken to this variety like it has to Chardonnay. Some winemakers have even employed a heavy-handed oaking to make Sauvignon Blanc seem more like Chardonnay. Fortunately, low demand has kept the prices down somewhat.

Riesling

Main growing regions: Germany, Austria, Alsace (France), Washington, New York's Finger Lakes district, and California

Aromas and flavors: Apricots, citrus, peaches, and flowers

Acidity: Moderate to high

Body: Light; medium to heavy for dessert wines

Major mixing partners: None (Riesling is often blended with lesser varieties in nonvarietal German QbA wines.)

Just as Pinot Noir rivals Cabernet Sauvignon for pre-eminence among noble red varieties, the Riesling grape has a following that regards it as superior to Chardonnay. Like Pinot Noir, Riesling has not traveled as well as its rival. Both Pinot Noir and Riesling turn shy in the warmth of California and require a cooler climate in order to perform well. Whereas the demand for quality Pinot Noir has motivated American winemakers to seek out promising vineyards for growing it, Riesling has never been in high demand in the United States.

Suggested Food Pairings

Drier versions are good with seafood, particularly shellfish. Riesling served with lobster is a very good match.

Perhaps if Riesling had been widely planted in France it would have found its niche in French gastronomy and secured its immortality. However, Riesling is only permitted to grow in French soil in the Alsace region of France.

In general, the aroma of well-made Riesling is flowery as well as fruity, and Riesling smells sweeter than Chardonnay. In fact, Riesling's alleged sweetness has kept it out of the fast lane in today's wine market. While it is true that Riesling grapes can make sweet wine—their prominent acidity provides the perfect balance for late-harvest sweetness, and they can produce the sweetest dessert wines in the world—some other excellent Rieslings, notably those from Alsace and Austria, can be nearly bone dry.

Riesling has long been the basis for the finest wines of Germany. The steep slopes along the Rhine and Mosel rivers retain warmth and incubate the Riesling to full ripeness in the otherwise chilly climate. Attaining the sweetness needed to become a good dessert wine in such a northerly climate is quite a victory over nature.

Although the Semillon-based dessert wines from Sauternes, France, are equally noteworthy as world-class dessert wines, these wines need some acidic Sauvignon Blanc blended in to balance the flaccid sweetness of *botrytis*-affected Semillon. Sweet Riesling need not be blended.

Some of the best values in the wine world today are the German Rieslings designated QbA (*Qualitätswein bestimmter Anbaugebiete*, or "quality wine") and labeled "Riesling." The superior QmP (*Qual-itätswein mit Prädikat*, or "highest quality") white wines from Germany are, by definition, made from Riesling unless labeled otherwise.

There have been some notable successes with Riesling in North America, many outside of California. Oregon, Washington State, Idaho, New York State, and Canada all produce quality Rieslings.

Be wary of imitations! Several lowly grape varieties, including Gray Riesling and Welschriesling, are deceptively named and have nothing to do with the real thing. Look for wines labeled "Riesling," "White Riesling," or "Johannisberg Riesling." Don't be afraid of an older bottle. Rieslings have demonstrated a capacity to improve with age, much more so than Chardonnays. This is especially true of the Alsace and German Rieslings.

Recommended Riesling

Name	Region	Price
St.-Urbans-Hof QbA	Mosel-Saar-Ruwer, Germany	$12
Dr. Konstantin Frank "Semi-Dry"	Finger Lakes, NY	$15
Kurt Darting Dürkheimer Michelsberg Kabinett 2002	Pfalz, Germany	$16
J. Haart, Piesporter Goldtröpfchen Kabinett 2002	Mosel, Germany	$18
Château St. Michelle-Dr. Loosen "Eroica"	Washington State	$20
Schloss Johannisberger QbA 2002	Rheingau, Germany	$22
Nikolaihof "Federspiel"	Wachau, Austria	$23
Domaine Weinbach "Réserve Personnelle"	Alsace, France	$25
J. J. Prüm, Wehlener Sonnenuhr Spätlese 2002	Mosel, Germany	$30
Grosset "Polish Hill"	Clare Valley, Australia	$30

Chenin Blanc

Main growing regions: Loire (France), South Africa, New
    Zealand, and California
Aromas and flavors: Somewhat muted; melon, honey
Acidity: Often very high
Body: Light to medium
Major mixing partner: Sometimes blended with Chardonnay
    in the Loire region

Chenin Blanc is widely grown around the world and has several distinct personalities. In the Loire Valley of Northwestern France, where it has been cultivated for over a thousand years, Chenin Blanc is responsible for the acidic white wines of Anjou and Touraine. The best known of these is Vouvray, which itself can take several forms.

Vouvray, whose name comes from the village in Touraine where it is produced, is the most weather-sensitive table wine. Whereas winemakers elsewhere usually attempt to produce a consistent style from vintage to vintage, Vouvray is made in different styles depending on the weather. A pleasant, sunny summer brings the Chenin Blanc grapes in Vouvray to full ripeness. In such years demi-sec (half-dry) wine is produced. A cold and rainy summer is unwelcome in any vineyard. Rather than gnash their teeth, though, winemakers respond by making Vouvray sec. This dry version of Chenin Blanc is very acidic. Vouvray sec has a following among connoisseurs who prize naked acidity. On the other end of the sweetness spectrum is Quarts de Chaume, a melony, honeyed dessert wine made from *botrytis*-affected Chenin Blanc from Anjou in the Loire Valley. These sweet wines are said to live indefinitely in the bottle, as do the sweeter versions of the Vouvray demi-sec.

High acidity is the backbone of well-made sparkling wine, and the naturally acidic Chenin Blanc grape is used to make high-quality sparkling wine in the Loire region. Semi-sparkling wine labeled "Vouvray Mousseux" is common, and the great Champagne firm of Taittinger produces its Bouvet Brut from Chenin Blanc in the Loire. These sparkling wines, though not as complex as true Champagne, are often made just as well and offer excellent value.

Chenin Blanc has traveled abroad with success. It was brought to South Africa in the 1600s by Dutch settlers and is widely grown there under the name of Steen. In California, Chenin Blanc is extensively cultivated for use in brandy-making and as part of the mix in jug wines. Chenin Blanc is capable of retaining its acidity at high yields and in high temperatures, a quality that makes it an economically important variety for high-volume production.

There have also been many pleasant and enjoyable California Chenin Blancs sold as varietal wines, but their popularity is fading. The best of these display the same honey and melon aromas as

Suggested Food Pairings

In general, Chenin Blanc–based wines match well with summer foods. Because of their high acidity, restrained fruit, and balance, well-made versions can be a welcome respite from your usual white wine. These wines have a natural affinity with sweet shellfish like sea scallops, but are also enjoyable with anything light, such as pasta, fish, and chicken.

Demi-sec wines have a pleasant level of residual sugar, but they are dry enough to enjoy with dinner. Chenin Blanc's inherent bracing acidity provides ample balance to the sweetness in demi-sec wines. These wines match well with a wide variety of light dishes. Vouvray sec is difficult to enjoy without food and is best matched with fresh shellfish.

Quarts-de-Chaume with moderate acidity—perfect summer wines. In addition to its use in California jug wines, Chenin Blanc is sometimes blended with Chardonnay in New Zealand and in Loire.

Recommended Chenin Blanc

Name	Region	Price
S. A. Huët "Le Haut-Lieu" Vouvray Demi-Sec	Loire Valley, France	$25
Marc Brédif Vouvray	Loire Valley, France	$13
Chappellet "Old Vine Cuvée"	Napa Valley, CA	$15
Mulderbosch	Stellenbosch, South Africa	$15
Domaine des Baumard Quarts-de-Chaume 2000 (375ml)	Loire Valley, France	$30

Pinot Blanc

Main growing regions: Burgundy (France), Alsace (France), Italy, Austria, and California

Aromas and flavors: Somewhat subdued, almonds and apples

Acidity: Moderate to high

Body: Medium to full

Major mixing partner: Rarely blended; formerly with Chardonnay in Burgundy

Also known as Pinot Bianco in Italy, Pinot Blanc is recognized for its simple, full-bodied, clean structure and forward acidity. It is used (in combination with other grapes) for some premium sparkling wines in California. Not widely produced in California, Pinot Blanc can be a good value among Alsace wines.

Originally grown in ancient Burgundy, Pinot Blanc has long been cultivated side by side with Chardonnay. Indeed, some mutations of

Pinot Blanc are capable of producing a Chardonnay-like wine. But for the most part, Pinot Blanc makes a rather nondescript wine with weak aroma. More than any other grape variety, Pinot Blanc can make a perfect "background wine," one that knows how to let elaborately flavored foods be the star of the dinner.

Recommended Pinot Blanc

Name	Region	Price
Alois Lageder Pinot Bianco	Trentino-Alto Adige, Italy	$10
Polz Weissburgunder	Südsteiermark, Austria	$15
Colterenzio Pinot Bianco "Weisshaus"	Trentino-Aldo Adige, Italy	$15
Paul Blanck "Pinot Blanc d'Alsace"	Alsace, France	$15
Steele	Santa Barbara, CA	$17

Semillon

Main growing regions: Bordeaux (France), Australia, and California
Aromas and flavors: Figs, honey, and lemon
Acidity: Low to medium
Body: Full
Major mixing partners: Sauvignon Blanc (Bordeaux)

The Semillon grape rarely stands alone as a varietal. It is often blended in the Graves subregion of Bordeaux, France, with Sauvignon

Blanc. Its silky richness is offset perfectly by the complementary acidity of Sauvignon Blanc. Semillon is the main variety in Sauternes, the dessert wine-producing subregion of Bordeaux. These wines also have Sauvignon Blanc mixed in to give them a little acidity. Good and affordable dessert Semillon, in its pure form, is produced in Australia.

Its signature characteristics are low acidity and thick body, and its aromas and flavors of figs, honey, and lemon are restrained. This set of qualities does not add up to an exceptional table wine, although good, inexpensive varietal Semillon is available. However, Semillon's propensity for richness and its susceptibility to "noble rot" make it a useful grape variety, albeit one with limited applications.

Recommended Semillon

Name	Region	Price
Australian Peter Lehmann Botrytis Semillon (375ml)	Barossa Valley, Australia	$13
Beringer "Alluvium" White	Knights Valley, Sonoma, CA	$17
Brokenwood	Lower Hunter Valley, Australia	$20
L'Ecole No. 41 "Seven Hills Estate"	Walla Walla Valley, WA	$23

Viognier

Main growing regions: Rhône (France) and California
Aromas and flavors: Apricots, wood, peaches, and flowers
Acidity: Low to medium
Body: Medium to full
Major mixing partners: None

The long-unheralded Viognier grape has been producing some fine alternatives to Chardonnay in France's upper Rhône. Viognier's popularity is fairly recent as a varietal from California. Its apricot/ peach flavors are a refreshing alternative to the perhaps repetitive pear/vanilla flavors of California Chardonnay. In fact, Viognier's biggest asset may be its vastly different flavor structure compared to Chardonnay, making it a good choice for those seeking an alternative to the latter.

The Northern Rhône valley of Condrieu is Viognier's home turf. The smallest recognized appellation in France is Château Grillet, a single estate within Condrieu. The Viognier grape approaches world-class status at this tiny property: A bottle of Château Grillet fetches $100 or more, and it is said to age well forever in the bottle. Less expensive but certainly noteworthy versions of Viognier come from the surrounding Condrieu vineyards.

California Viognier is not any cheaper than Chardonnay. For bargains, look for varietal Viognier from big French producers. Inexpensive *vin de pays* varietal Viognier has caught on in the French countryside, at least for export. These wines are often good values in terms of quality when compared with similarly priced Chardonnay.

Suggested Food Pairings

At its best, Viognier has aromas and flavors of peach, apricot, and flowers, though it is not as overtly flowery as Riesling. With the aromas and flavors of these particular fruits, Viognier is a natural match with pork, which has an affinity for both. However, if you substitute Viognier for Chardonnay in any food-wine pairing, you won't be disappointed.

Recommended Viognier

Name	Region	Price
Château Pesquie	Côtes-du-Ventoux, Rhône, France	$13
Zaca Mesa	Santa Ynez, CA	$14
Alban	Central Coast, CA	$20
Jaffurs	Santa Barbara, CA	$23
Guigal Condrieu	Rhone, France	$45

Pinot Grigio/Pinot Gris

Main growing regions: Italy, Alsace, Oregon, and California
Aromas and flavors: Somewhat muted; minerals, pine, and
    orange rind
Acidity: Medium (generally higher in Europe)
Body: Medium (generally heavier in the United States)
Major mixing partners: None

A close relative of Pinot Blanc, Pinot Grigio has recently become a very popular varietal wine from Italy. In Friuli and Aldo Adige, two Northern regions of Italy, Pinot Grigio can produce a well-structured and acidic match for seafood, with somewhat muddled aromas. In warmer climates, however, the acidity level can be undesirably low. Pinot Grigio is a relatively recent visitor to California, where it has yet to succeed in making wines comparable to those in Northern Italy.

Alsatian soil brings out the best in several white varieties, and Pinot Grigio, known there as Tokay Pinot Gris, is one of them. This pink-skinned variety is not strong-willed and is a perfect vehicle for the Alsace *terroir*—rich, minerally soil flavors mingle with the acidity.

The Oregonians call their version Pinot Gris. The cool Willamette Valley appears to be a Pinot Gris–friendly growing region. These wines have stronger than usual Pinot Gris flavor, rich body,

Suggested Food Pairings

Because it doesn't have prominent fruit flavors, Pinot Grigio is relatively easy to match with food. The drier, more acidic versions are excellent with shell-fish and other seafoods, whereas the fuller-bodied versions can accompany chicken and pasta dishes well.

and the signature citrus aromas of Pinot Grigio. These wines tend to be more expensive than the Italian versions.

Recommended Pinot Gris/Pinot Grigio

Name	Region	Price
Pighin, Grave del Friuli	Friuli, Italy	$13
Willamette Valley Vineyards	Oregon	$15
Trimbach Reserve	Alsace, France	$16
King Estate "Reserve"	Oregon	$20
Maso Poli	Trentino-Alto Adige, Italy	$20
Jermann	Friuli, Italy	$30
Domaine Zind-Humbrecht "Clos Windsbuhl"	Alsace, France	$55

Gewürztraminer

Main growing regions: Germany, Alsace (France), and California

Aromas and flavors: Strong lychee-nut fruit, rose petal, and grapefruit rind

Acidity: Low to medium

Body: Full

Major mixing partners: None

Gewürztraminer (pronounced gah-VERTS-truh-MEEN-er) is a pink-skinned clone of the much older Traminer vine that probably originated in Northern Italy. "Gewürz-" is German for "spicy" or "pungent" and reflects the powerful aromas of Gewürztraminer wines. It is the least subtle of all the well-known *vinifera* grapes.

Although it grows best in Alsace (France), it plays second fiddle there to the Riesling grape. Its share of vineyard space in Germany has been on the decline, again being out-muscled by the Riesling grape. California and Pacific Northwest versions of this quirky variety tend to lack the complexity of their European counterparts, but can be both enjoyable and affordable.

Recommended Gewürztraminer

Name	Region	Price
Standing Stone	Finger Lakes, NY	$19
Martinelli	Russian River Valley, Sonoma, CA	$20
Navarro	Mendocino, CA	$25
Domaine Zind-Humbrecht "Turkheim"	Alsace, France	$30
Domaine Weinbach "Cuvée St. Catherine"	Alsace, France	$50

Suggested Food Pairings

Rich, pungent, spicy flavors with fruit notes of lychee and grapefruit rind make for a difficult food-wine pairing. As such, Gewürztraminer is often suggested with spicy Asian food—an awkward blind date at best. Regional tradition in Alsace matches Gewürztraminer with sausage and ham. Because of its low acidity and bold flavors, Gewürztraminer can be enjoyable without food. Alternatively, a simple, creamy cheese provides a good background for the complex, full personality of this grape.

Grüner Veltliner

Major growing areas: Eastern Austria
Aromas and Flavors: Green beans, lentils, and ground pepper
Acidity: Moderate
Body: Medium to full
Major mixing partners: None

This once obscure grape variety has risen to prominence in the last decade for two reasons—the wines of Austria are usually very well made, and Grüner Veltliner is quite food-friendly. One well-known wine importer described Grüner Veltliner as tasting like the offspring of Riesling and Sauvignon Blanc.

Recommended Grüner Veltliner

Name	Region	Price
Glatzer	Carnuntum, Austria	$12
Familie Nigl "Kremser Freiheit"	Kremstal, Austria	$17
R & A Pfaffl "Goldjoch"	Weinviertel, Austria	$19
Bründlmayer "Alte Reben"	Kamptal, Austria	$45
Nikolaihof Smaragd Trocken	Wachau, Austria	$50

Suggested Food Pairings

Grüner Veltliner has caught on recently among wine stewards and their more savvy clientele because it is compatible with so many dishes—even well-known wine-killers such as asparagus and artichokes. Grüner Veltliner often shows up on wine lists in upscale Asian restaurants, particularly Vietnamese, where it is nicely paired with dishes seasoned with lemongrass and the other powerful and pungent seasonings characteristic of that cuisine.

Chapter 9

Wine Regions

THREE SHORT DECADES AGO, there was little to discuss about wine regions outside of France, other than the Napa Valley, perhaps, where some brash young upstarts had demonstrated California's potential. What about German wine? A long and proud tradition to be sure, but too *sweet*. (Not necessarily true, then or today.) And what to do with Italian wine? Drink it with spaghetti and stick a candle in the empty. (It is true that back in the 1970s, the Italian wine industry was still being dragged, kicking and screaming, into the twentieth century.) South American wine cost about $2 and just gave you a headache . . . it was only a slight improvement over Mexican tap water. Australian wine? Banana juice! (This country's early efforts had a lot more fruit than acidity.) And forget South African Wine—that country was politically embargoed right out of the wine boom until the 1990s. New Zealand wine wasn't happening yet. And as for Spanish wine, it was good for making sangria, maybe. (Some old-style Spanish reds were aged for a decade in oak casks, robbing them of any fruit whatsoever.)

The wine world has changed considerably in the past thirty years. Scientific progress led to the large-scale modernization of commercial winemaking, which then made it possible to update traditional wine regions and develop new and promising sites all over the globe. Adventurous wine lovers can now enjoy high-quality wines from some twenty different nations whose wares usually reflect in some way the old European wine traditions and styles while also imparting some unique twists of their own.

The Home of the Vine

The wine grape thrives in weather conditions that are neither too hot nor too cold. Too much heat rushes the grapes to ripeness without allowing for full flavor development and then scorches their skins brown. A lack of adequate heat is also detrimental; it prevents grapes from ripening sufficiently, and fine wine production thus becomes economically, if not physically, impossible. The wine grape prefers moderate warmth, spread over seven or more frost-free months. Winter must be cold enough to draw the vines into dormancy, yet not much colder than that; even the hardiest *vinifera* stock cannot withstand a brutal, subzero cold snap without significant physiological damage. And so the primary determinant of a wine region's viability is the range of its temperatures over the course of the year.

Climate Conditions

As previously noted in this book, the ancient Greeks maintained that the realm of the wine grape was limited to that of the fig and the olive—a warm climate, indeed, not too far from the Mediterranean sea. When the Romans pushed this arbitrary boundary northward into continental Europe, they demonstrated that viticulture was not only possible, it was even preferable, in cooler European climates as far north as the evergreen oak could thrive.

The wine regions of the world are found generally between the 30th and 50th degrees parallel, with certain exceptions. Quality viticulture is possible closer to the equator, in mountainous regions where the high altitude approximates the cooler conditions farther from the equator. Extreme northerly (or southerly) viticulture may be possible as well, when specific weather conditions—such as the Northeast Atlantic gulf stream or the alpine *fohn* (the warm downhill wind)—bring late-season warmth to the vineyards. Thus the *macroclimate*, the wine region's long-term, general weather pattern, is a prerequisite for fine wine production.

Ideal Soil

The wine grape, like all plants, needs water, but prefers dry climates to dampness. Rainfall is welcome in the springtime, but not right before the harvest, when it can swell the grapes and dilute the wine. Soils that easily drain themselves of moisture are ideal, and the soils of the great wine regions in the world are usually known for their stone and mineral content rather than their richness. The vineyard "soil" of the Châteauneuf-du-Pape region, for instance, is made up mostly of saucer-shaped white stones—*galettes*—that reflect the sun's rays toward the vines by day and release their stored energy at night, thus bringing the vines to a level of ripeness unmatched elsewhere in France. It is a great anomaly of viticulture that the grape vine—unlike almost every other cash crop on the planet—grows best in soils nearly devoid of biological nutrients.

Within the macroclimates bathed with appropriate amounts of warmth and sunshine, there are smaller pockets of land blessed with ideal soils for grape cultivation and shielded, one way or another, from excessive rains. Sometimes a local geographic feature—such as a south-facing hillside that easily gathers sunshine, or a deep river valley that holds autumn warmth a little later into the season—can result in a certain piece of land producing wines of particular distinction. This is known as a *microclimate*.

And so we have the elements of a successful wine region: macroclimate, microclimate, and soil. Taken together, these are known to the French as *terroir*—the set of climatic and geological qualities unique to a particular piece of land. It is because of this notion of *terroir* that the French and other European wine producers have long considered a wine's geographic origin to be of foremost importance, more important even than grape variety.

Against this backdrop, let us go on a tour of the wine-producing regions of the world.

France

France is the mother lode of fine wine, perfectly situated as it is along the sun-drenched Mediterranean and the balmy Atlantic Gulf Stream, and sliced by long river valleys that channel warmth to her inland vines. Nature's unparalleled gifts notwithstanding, it was through arduous trial and error that the French learned how to make very good wine. This ability developed only after centuries of careful cultivation and meticulous record-keeping, particularly by the Church.

Indeed, it is not farfetched to say that the French have defined quality wine for the rest of the world. The wineries of California,

South America, and Australia all strive to produce wine that will compare favorably with French wines, as if those were the gold standard. These New-World regions, especially California, may have succeeded in producing beautiful wines that often exceed their French counterparts in sheer power, but they rarely match the French wines when it comes to finesse.

It is generally accepted among wine experts that France produces many "best-of" wine types:

- The *tête-de-cuvée* Champagnes from the top houses are the finest sparkling wines in the world. Alsace Gewürztraminer is the best version of this quirky wine.
- The Haut-Médoc subregion of Bordeaux produces, in its greatest years, the finest Cabernet Sauvignon–based wines in the world.
- Merlot best displays its qualities in the Bordeaux subregions of Saint-Emilion and Pomerol.
- The *grand cru* vineyards of the Côte de Beaune produce the finest Chardonnays on Earth.
- The most refined Sauvignon Blanc–based wines are produced in the upper Loire subregions of Sancerre and Pouilly-Fumé, and the Graves subregion of Bordeaux.
- Chenin Blanc is in its glory along the middle Loire River.
- Sauternes, from the town of the same name, is widely acclaimed as the world's finest dessert wine.
- The prototype for world-class Pinot Noir comes from the vineyards of Côte de Nuits in Burgundy.
- For a simple, acidic shellfish wine, Muscadet is unparalleled.
- Finally, the dry rosé wines of Provence are considered to be the best of their type.

Except for those varietal wines aimed directly at the American market, French wines are usually labeled by geographical region (e.g., Bordeaux) rather than grape variety. This reflects the French view that geographic origin—*terroir*—is of supreme importance in producing quality wines. Other than inexpensive, varietally labeled *vin de pays* (country wine), only the wines from the Alsace region are labeled by their grape variety.

In order to understand the degrees of specificity of French wine labeling, think of an archery target. The outer circle is all of France; the next-largest circle is a region of France such as Bordeaux; the next circle is in the district of, say, Médoc; within that is the commune name—Pauillac, for instance; finally, the bull's eye is the individual producer, a château or domain. The better (and more expensive) the wine, the more specific the indicated source of the wine will be.

Just as French society is hierarchical—sometimes ridiculously so—so is her classification of her beloved wines. A general understanding of the classification of French wine is vital to your wine knowledge, since France long ago invented the wines that the rest of the world imitates. (Even the bottle shapes of the different wine styles and wine regions of France are imitated by California winemakers to indicate the intended style of wine.)

Label law is of particular importance to the classification of French wine. Following is a breakdown of the most important labeling designations from France:

- **Appellation d'Origine Contrôlée (AOC or AC):** This is the most widely applied standard used on French wine labels. It indicates that the wine meets the legal standards (per French wine law) for the area indicated. The more specific the area of origin, the higher the standards.

- **Vins Délimités de Qualité Supérieure (VDQS):** This second set of standards is used for wines in areas not covered by AOC law. Although wines labeled as such are a notch lower in quality, VDQS is still a reliable government guarantee.
- *Vin de Pays*: This indicates "country" wine from outlying areas. Most varietal wines (those wines where the name of the grape is on the bottle) fall under this heading. Sometimes a wine from an AOC may be "declassified" to a *vin de pays* in order to meet government regulations pertaining to maximum crop yields. Such a wine, often priced well under $10, is usually a terrific bargain.

In order to understand France's system of wine production, think of the country in terms of its seven major regions. Each of these regions has its own system of organization and classification:

Bordeaux
Burgundy (Bourgogne)
Rhône
Loire

Alsace
Languedoc
Champagne

Bordeaux

Bordeaux, an industrial city in Southwestern France, is the center of the world's most famous wine region. Several types of wine are produced here:

- **Dry white wines:** These include blends of Sauvignon Blanc and Semillon.

- **Sweet dessert wines:** This encompasses blends of Sauvignon Blanc, Semillon, and Muscadelle afflicted with *botrytis cinerea* (noble rot), the grape mold that concentrates the natural sugars.
- **Medium-bodied red wines:** This classification is comprised of blends of Cabernet Sauvignon, Merlot, Cabernet Franc, Malbec, and Petit Verdot. Some subregions produce wine made primarily from Cabernet Sauvignon, whereas the Merlot grape is dominant in other areas.

There are several subregions of Bordeaux that produce particular types of wine. Here are the most important:

- **Sauternes:** sweet dessert wines
- **Pomerol:** Merlot-dominant reds
- **Saint-Emilion:** Merlot-dominant reds, blended with a significant amount of Cabernet Franc
- **Entre-Deux-Mers:** light, simple whites
- **Graves:** fine dry whites, Cabernet Sauvignon–based reds
- **Médoc:** Cabernet Sauvignon–based reds

The Médoc, a subregion of Bordeaux, is a relatively large area and contains four "communes" (wine-producing areas that are like small towns). These communes are entitled to their own appellation:

Saint-Estèphe   Margaux
Saint-Julien   Pauillac

You will find a great number of châteaux-bottled Bordeaux wines on the market. A château is literally a piece of land. In anticipation of an agricultural exposition in 1855, the local government in Bordeaux asked representatives of the wine trade to rate the red wines of Médoc according to price history. Those wines that had fetched the highest prices over time were given the highest ranking, and so on down. The highest ranking, *premier cru* ("first growth"), includes only five (originally four) châteaux, one of which (Château Haut-Brion) is actually from neighboring Graves. This château was included because of its record of excellence. The classified growths of Médoc are ranked first growth, second, third, fourth, and fifth. Below this level are the *cru bourgeois* wines and the *petits châteaux* wines.

The sweet dessert wines of Sauternes were classified at the time of those of Médoc. Other subregions of Bordeaux have since adopted some form of classification. Although such quality classifications might become outdated and might no longer reflect reality, they can be self-fulfilling prophecies: A *premier cru* is expected to be expensive and excellent; therefore, the winemaker can afford to make such a wine, knowing that the market will accept the price.

Burgundy (Bourgogne)

This region begins approximately 62 miles (100 kilometers) south of Paris and stretches about 224 miles (360 kilometers) down to Lyon. Burgundy produces three general types of wine:

1.   Light, velvety red wine made from Pinot Noir.
2.   Light, fruity red wine made from Gamay.
3.   Dry white wine made from Chardonnay.

Although there are other wines made in Burgundy, these are the most important.

If you were to travel from north to south through the heart of France, you would pass through the following subregions of Burgundy in sequence:

- **Chablis:** This subregion produces very dry white wines.
- **Côte de Nuits:** This area is home to full-bodied Pinot Noir reds and also a few whites.
- **Côte de Beaune:** This section is known for its lighter Pinot Noir and excellent Chardonnay.
- **Côte Chalonnaise:** Less expensive Pinot Noir and Chardonnay is produced in this subregion.
- **Mâcon:** Chardonnay whites, including the famous Pouilly-Fuissé, are produced here.
- **Beaujolais:** Gamay reds come from this part of Burgundy.

Many of these subregions have their own ranking systems. For instance, the Chablis vineyards are ranked (in descending order of quality) as Chablis *Grand Cru*, Chablis *Premier Cru*, Chablis, and Petit Chablis. The red and white vineyards of the Côte de Nuits and Côte de Beaune (together known as the Côte d'Or) are ranked either *Grand Cru* or *Premier Cru*, although sometimes they are not ranked at all.

Some of Burgundy's subregions break down further into other sections. For example, the famous villages of the Côte de Nuits are Nuits-Saint-Georges; Gevrey-Chambertin; Vosne-Romanée; Morey-Saint-Denis; and Chambolle-Musigny. These villages are all well-known for their red wines, some of which are fabulously expensive.

The Côte de Beaune encompasses an even greater number of renowned villages, known for producing either red or white wine. According to wine type, these are:

Reds

Pernand-Vergelesses	Pommard
Savigny-les-Beaune	Beaune
Volnay	Meursault

Whites

Puligny-Montrachet	Beaune
Chassagne-Montrachet	Aloxe-Corton
Meursault	

Beaujolais is the southernmost subregion of Burgundy. However, the Pinot Noir grape of the Côte d'Or (and Côte Chalonnaise) gives way to the Gamay grape, which produces charming wines in Beaujolais' granite-rich soil.

The wines of Beaujolais may be labeled as Beaujolais, Beaujolais Supérieur (which is 1 percent higher in alcohol content than simple Beaujolais), Beaujolais-Villages, or *cru* Beaujolais with a village name. Moulin-à-Vent, Brouilly, and St-Amour are the best known of the *crus*. There are ten such *cru* villages entitled to use their own names. *Cru* Beaujolais is the best of the Beaujolais and, since it usually costs less than $15 a bottle, it's quite a bargain!

Rhône

Earthy, gutsy wines, both red and white, are produced along the Rhône River, which lies south of the Burgundy region. Mercifully, the wines of the Rhône region do not have a ranking system.

Northern Rhône reds include:

Big, Syrah-based reds worthy of aging for at least a few years.
Côte Rôtie
Hermitage-Crozes-Hermitage
Cornas
St. Joseph

Northern Rhône whites are substantial wines made from Viognier or a blend of Marsanne and Roussane. These include:

 Condrieu
Hermitage-Crozes-Hermitage

The following red wines are produced in Southern Rhône:

Grenache-based blends (with Syrah, Cinsault, Mouvédre,
and other grapes)
Côtes-du-Rhône
Gigondas
Châteauneuf-du-Pape

Although not so common, Southern Rhône whites are big wines made from Marsanne and Roussane. These wines are an interesting alternative to Chardonnay:

Côtes-du-Rhône Blanc
Châteauneuf-du-Pape Blanc

The Southern Rhône region also produces a distinguished rosé known as Tavel. This dry rosé, made primarily from Grenache, is considered by many wine buffs to be the finest rosé in the world.

Loire

The vineyards along the largest river in France yield a variety of refreshing (mostly white) wines. Here are the most important ones:

- **Muscadet:** a perfect shellfish wine, it is made from the grape of the same name.
- **Vouvray:** Produced from the Chenin Blanc grape, Vouvray can be bone-dry (sec), delightfully off-dry (demi-sec), or sparkling.
- **Rosé d'Anjou**: This off-dry rosé is made mostly from the Grolleau grape, while superior rosés from the region made from Cabernet Sauvignon and Cabernet Franc are labeled Cabernet d'Anjou.
- **Pouilly-Fumé:** A straight Sauvignon Blanc with a rich, heady style, this wine is the inspiration for California Sauvignon Blancs labeled "Fumé Blanc."
- **Sancerre:** This unblended Sauvignon Blanc is more acidic than Pouilly-Fumé.

Alsace

Historically, ownership of the geographical area of Alsace has flip-flopped back and forth between Germany and France, according to which country claimed victory in the most recent war. As such, although Alsace is currently a part of France, considerable German influence is, nevertheless, apparent in this region's wines. Late harvest, sweet wines are produced in Alsace.

In this region there is a tradition of varietal labeling: No "cutting" is allowed. If a wine is named according to grape variety, then it must be made only from that grape. The term *grand cru* may appear on an Alsace label as an indication that the wine has a minimum alcohol content of 10 or 11 percent (depending on the grape) and meets some perfunctory yield requirements. The varieties used in Alsace wines are:

Riesling
Gewürztraminer
Pinot Gris (Tokay Pinot Gris)
Muscat

Sylvaner
A small amount of Pinot
    Noir (the only red,
    often used for rosé)

Champagne

In order to qualify for the Champagne appellation (according to French and EEC law), a sparkling wine must:

1. Be produced in the Champagne district
2. Be produced from the Chardonnay, Pinot Noir, and/or Pinot Meunier (red) grapes grown there
3. Get its bubbles via the méthode champenoise (Champagne method)

The Champagne method is an expensive and labor-intensive means of naturally carbonating a wine. First, wine is made from local grapes. This is no easy feat; the vineyards of Champagne lie so far north that ripeness is an issue in most years. After clarification and aging, the wine is put into thick Champagne bottles, along with enough yeast and sugar to initiate a second fermentation. It is this second fermentation in the tightly sealed bottle that puts the bubbles in the bubbly—the carbon dioxide cannot escape, so it is dissolved in the wine.

Then comes the hard work—removing the dead yeast. After aging the wine with the dead yeast—sometimes for many years, as this adds character to the Champagne—the dead yeast is then coaxed into the neck of the bottle by gradually tilting the bottle a little bit each day until it is inverted. The dead yeast is then carefully removed. At this time, the bottle is topped off and adjusted for sweetness. Champagnes can vary significantly in terms of sweetness, and the amount of sugar is noted on the bottle's label. Following are the distinctions used to indicate Champagne's sweetness:

- **Natural or Au Sauvage** indicates no sugar has been added.
- **Brut** is the designation used for very dry Champagne, that contains no more than 1.5 percent sugar by volume.
- **Extra Dry** Champagne contains up to 2 percent sugar.
- **Dry or Sec** Champagne contains up to 4 percent sugar.
- **Demi-Sec** Champagne is sweeter, with as much as 8 percent sugar.
- **Doux** Champagne is very sweet and consists of up to 10 percent sugar.

When considering champagne, there are some other important terms with which you should be familiar. These include:

- **Blanc de Blancs:** This term indicates that a champagne is made only from white grapes, such as Chardonnay.
- **Brut Rosé:** This is a designation used for pink-colored Champagne. The color is derived from the red skins of Pinot Noir and/or Pinot Meunier grapes.
- **Blanc de Noirs:** Pale sparkling wine from dark-skinned grapes goes by this label.

- **Téte de Cuvée:** This term is used to distinguish a super-premium Champagne, usually vintage dated.
- **Vintage:** In contrast to the far more common practice of blending wines from different years, vintage Champagne is made from the wine of a single harvest. Although most téte de cuvées are vintage dated, a year on the bottle doesn't mean that it is superior to a nonvintage bottle.

Italy

For a beginning wine lover becoming familiar with the wines of France and their Californian counterparts, the world of Italian wine can be a tough nut to crack. Although the wines of the United States can be explained in relationship to their French counterparts (and *vice versa*), the wines of Italy cannot. The land we now call Italy has been producing wine for 4,000 years; however, Italy was not politically unified within its present borders until the mid-1800s. This land of diverse climates, cultures, and dialects produces a baffling variety of wines.

The wines of Italy rival those of France in variety, quantity, and, in many cases, quality. Like France, Italy more often than not labels her wines according to geographical origin rather than grape variety. (Of course, as with France, there are exceptions.) Italy is divided politically into twenty regions: From south to north, these include:

Calabria (the "toe")	Abruzzo
Apulia (*Puglia* in Italian, also known as the "heel")	Latium (*Lazio*)
	Umbria
Basilicata	Marche
Campania	Tuscany (*Toscana*)
Molise	Emilia-Romagna

In the north, there are also several regions along the French, Swiss, Austrian, and Slovenian borders. These are:

Liguria
Piedmont (*Piemonte*)
Valle d'Aosta
Lombardy (*Lombardia*)

Trentino-Alto Adige
Veneto
Friuli-Venezia Giulia

There are two island regions as well:

Sicily (*Sicilia*, right off the coast of the Calabria region)
Sardinia (about 200 miles off the coast of the Latium region)

Sardinia and Sicily

Italy is a wine-loving country, and every one of these regions produces wine. The island region of Sardinia, for instance, which is dedicated primarily to other forms of agriculture such as sheep and cattle, nonetheless produces interesting wines. In particular, the white grape Vermentino yields a light and crisp hot-weather wine. Meanwhile, the other island region, Sicily, has half a million acres of vineyards and has traditionally produced a variety of powerful, deeply colored red wines as well as a few whites. Ample Sicilian sunshine and warmth encourage viticulture on hillsides not quite fertile or rainy enough for abundant cultivation of other crops, though Sicily is certainly a bountiful garden compared to cooler wine regions in Northern Europe. Presently, the Nero d'Avola grape, native to Sicily, is enjoying a renaissance in the hands of modern producers, and better-known grape varieties—even Chardonnay—have performed well.

Calabria and Apulia

Across the narrow strait of Messina, the sun-drenched Calabria region barely dabbles in viticulture, devoting its rocky terrain instead to other forms of agriculture such as olives, eggplants, and lemons. However, the neighboring Apulia region, with its minerally, vine-friendly terrain, is a far more important wine producing region, if only in quantity. Its vineyard acreage equals Sicily's, and Primitivo di Mandura—the Italian version of the Zinfandel grape—as well as the rustic, inexpensive Salice Salentino are two Apulian red wines that regularly appear in American wine stores.

Campania

The Campania region is the source of Southern Italy's finest wines. The Aglianico grape, also grown in the neighboring Basilicata region where it is bottled as Aglianico del Vulture, yields a fine red wine in Campania's volcanic hillsides. The finest vintages of Aglianico, when vinified by Campania's top producers in the Taurasi zone, are among the greatest wines of Italy. Less noble grapes, such as the white varieties Coda di Volpe and Greco and the red Piedirosso, also perform well in Campanian vineyards.

Abruzzo

The Abruzzo region, on Italy's east coast, produces an ocean of inexpensive red wine confusingly named Montepulciano d'Abruzzo. Here we have "Montepulciano" used as the name of a grape variety, while it is also the name of a famous wine district in the Tuscany region. Montepulciano d'Abruzzo, at $6 to $10 per bottle, has become the quintessential "pizza wine"; however, *riserva* bottlings, made from vineyards with old vines and severely limited yields, can approach the greatness of the more famous Italian treasures from Campania and the northern regions.

Umbria

The neighboring Umbria region in Central Italy has enjoyed relatively recent success with varietal Sangiovese and Merlot, while a high quality, indigenous red grape is bottled as Sagrantino di Montefalco, well-made versions of which will reward a decade of cellar aging. It's not hard to understand why Umbrian wine producers have developed an inferiority complex over the centuries—Umbria's neighbor to the northwest is Tuscany, one of the very finest wine regions in the world.

Tuscany

A tour of Tuscan wines begins in the Chianti district. Many wine drinkers associate Chianti with the cheap, straw-wrapped bottles of indifferent quality sold for many years in American wine stores. Today, these bottles are increasingly scarce. The Chianti region, famous for its food-friendly wine, has recently solidified its reputation as a fine wine–producing subregion of Tuscany. Here, the Sangiovese grape and its close relatives thrive in the calcium-rich soils and moderate climate. The Chianti area is divided into seven zones:

Chianti Classico

Chianti Colli Senesi

Chianti Rufina

Chianti Colli Aretini

Chianti Colline Pisane

Chianti Colli Fiorentini

Chianti Montalbano

Of these, only Classico, Rufina, and, perhaps, Colli Senesi can be readily found in wine stores. Wine labeled simply as "Chianti" might well be from an outlying vineyard in the district. To the south of the Chianti district, there are two other fine wine-producing areas: the towns of Montepulciano and Montalcino.

Super-Tuscan Wines

A Tuscan revolution began in the late 1960s and is still sending new ripples through the wine world. The coastal Tuscan town of Bolgheri enjoys warmth unknown even in Montalcino, and innovative wine producers recently planted Cabernet Sauvignon vines there. The results were stunning, and a new category of Tuscan wine was born: the "super-Tuscans." Today, there are many producers bottling either Sangiovese-Cabernet Sauvignon blends or, alternatively, purely "Bordeaux blends" of Cabernet Sauvignon, Cabernet Franc, and Merlot without any Sangiovese. ❧

The sandy, well-drained vineyards of Montepulciano yield a red wine known as Vino Nobile di Montepulciano, a Sangiovese-based wine somewhat richer than that produced in Chianti, due in part to Montepulciano's slightly warmer microclimate. In Montalcino, meanwhile, a microclimate even warmer and drier yet brings a sturdier clone of Sangiovese—the Sangiovese Grosso, or "Brunello" grape—to lush, full ripeness. This wine is bottled as Brunello di Montalcino. Both Vino Nobile di Montepulciano and Brunello di Montalcino have "little brothers"—Rosso di Montepulciano and Rosso di Montalcino. Easier to confuse with each other than with their older brothers, they are generally light-bodied and relatively inexpensive reds intended for early consumption.

The Northernmost Regions

The Italian regions in the foothills of the Alps are home to many grape varieties, some familiar and others barely known outside of their regions. The Trentino-Alto Adige region sits along the Austrian border. Though it is one region, Trentino is the southern, Italian-speaking part while German is spoken in Alto Adige. Considering its northerly latitude (46°N) the region is surprisingly warm, as warm air accumulates on the south side of the alps. As such, internationally known grape varieties—the usual suspects—ripen easily and can be produced in large quantities. Chardonnay, Pinot Nero (Pinot Noir), Cabernet Sauvignon, Merlot, Pinot Bianco, and the ubiquitous Pinot Grigio are among the seventeen varieties bottled by name, as are the lesser-known local red grapes Schiava, Lagrein, and Teroldego.

Likewise, the Friuli region, in northeastern Italy, can ripen a wide variety of *vinifera* grapes, albeit with a tilt in the direction of fresh, fruity whites produced in its geologically wine-friendly hillsides and plains. Meanwhile, the Veneto region, situated between Friuli and Trentino-Alto Adige, produces a diverse assortment of wines. Soave, Bardolino, Valpolicella, Prosecco . . . these names fill the Italian racks at the wine store, and they all come from the Veneto region, which is a close third behind Apulia and Sicily in total wine production.

Prosecco is a delightfully clean and crisp sparkler produced in bulk from the grape of the same name. It's widely available in the $8 to $12 range. The Veneto region produces a considerable amount of inexpensive wines labeled by grape variety. Just about every region in Italy, from Sicily to Friuli, bottles its own version of Pinot Grigio, and the Veneto certainly contributes its share.

The Piave river valley in eastern Veneto is an especially prolific source of inexpensive, varietal Merlot, as well as other varietals.

Soave, the best-known white wine of the Veneto region, is a blend based on the local Garganega grape. The house of Bolla made Soave something of a brand name in the 1970s with its mass-produced and mass-marketed version of the wine, yet there are several distinctive versions available from small producers. The Soave district's next-door neighbors, the Bardolino and Valpolicella districts, are hosts to similarly mass-produced reds. Both Bardolino and Valpolicella are made from blends of grapes featuring the Corvina grape. Their normally light body is a reflection of the high crop yields commonly associated with mass production. As with Soave, there are some intriguing, handcrafted counterexamples.

At the other end of the spectrum in the Valpolicella district of the Veneto region is Amarone, another of Italy's wine treasures. A relatively recent development in fine Italian wine, Amarone is made in the same district and from the same grapes as common Valpolicella. However, the grapes used for Amarone are dried on straw mats for up to four months, a process that reduces the grapes' water content and, thus, concentrates the sugars. The resulting wine is richly flavored and textured with an alcoholic content of perhaps 15 to 16 percent. Like others in the pantheon of great Italian wines, Amarone is capable of aging for several decades. Next to a rich and powerful Amarone, plain Valpolicella can seem downright watery. However, some Valpolicella producers referment their wine with sediment left over from Amarone fermentation. This method of "repassing" (*ripasso*) Valpolicella gives it additional richness and complexity.

Piedmont

Veneto's Amarone, along with Taurasi from Campania and the many excellent wines from Tuscany, have earned their place among the world's great wines. However, of Italy's twenty wine regions, most connoisseurs would agree that the very finest Italian wines come from Piedmont.

Nebbiolo is one of the noblest *vinifera* varieties, yet it accomplishes little beyond the borders of Piedmont. However, in the vineyards of Barolo and Barbaresco, the Nebbiolo grape attains a degree of greatness shared only with the world's finest examples of Cabernet Sauvignon, Pinot Noir, Syrah, and, perhaps, Sangiovese. Although there is a degree of geological diversity in the region, the Piedmontese soils in which Nebbiolo thrives are not unlike those in Burgundy, where Pinot Noir grows so beautifully. This soil has mixtures of limestone, clay, and, in some areas, a proportion of sandstone as well.

The Nebbiolo grape gets its name from *nebbia*, the autumn fog prevalent in Piedmont. The region's subalpine climate—hot summers and relatively mild autumn days—brings the Nebbiolo, as well as the lesser varieties, to ideal ripeness. While Nebbiolo is a late-ripening variety, the Barbera grape ripens a little earlier and yields a low-tannin, high-acid red with broad appeal. The Dolcetto grape, which ripens even earlier, makes an almost Beaujolais-like light red perfect for youthful consumption. Lesser-known native grape varieties include Brachetto, Freisa, and Grignolino.

While Piedmont is best known for its outstanding reds, the white Gavi, made from the native Cortese variety, is a crisp and minerally seafood wine not unlike a good Sauvignon Blanc. In contrast, the Arneis grape can produce a less acidic, overtly fruity white meant for early consumption.

Piedmont also produces a few different sparkling wines. The mass-produced Asti Spumante is known worldwide as a sweet and inexpensive alternative to more serious sparklers, while the more refined Moscato d'Asti is less alcoholic (only 5.5 percent) and less effervescent. It also has a red cousin: Brachetto d'Aqui is a sweet, low-alcohol, slightly sparkling red with an aroma of fresh strawberries as festive as Moscato d'Asti's floral Muscat scent.

The Italian government recognizes the traditional wines of Italy (as well as some newcomers) with a system similar to France:

- **Denominazione di Origine Controllata e Garantita (DOCG):** This is the highest status conferred on Italian wines. It guarantees that the wine is of a traditional style from its region; made from specified grape varieties grown at the proper crop levels; and aged for a specified period of time prior to release. For example, Brunello di Montalcino, a DOCG wine from Tuscany, must be made from the Sangiovese Grosso clone (a.k.a. "Brunello") of the Sangiovese grape and is aged for four years prior to release.
- **Denominazione di Origine Controllata (DOC):** This next-highest level is often found on "little brother" wines, such as Tuscany's Rosso di Montalcino, the "little brother" of Brunello di Montalcino.
- **Indicazione Geografica Tipica (IGT):** This is a category for wines, some of which might include innovative styles or varieties that do not conform to DOCG/DOC regulations. For example, this includes varietals such as Syrah from Tuscany. IGT wine labels must indicate the general region of origin.
- **Vino da Tavola (VdT):** "Table wine," just like the French *vin de table*, is the general category for non-DOC/DOCG wines of indistinct origin. Before the IGT category was instituted, the high-quality, innovative "super-Tuscan" wines were labeled as VdT wines.

Major Italian Wine Types

Color	Type of Wine	Region	Grape Varieties
Red	Barolo	Piedmont	Nebbiolo
Red	Barbaresco	Piedmont	Nebbiolo
Red	Valpolicella	Veneto	Corvina, Rondinella, and Molinara
Red	Amarone	Veneto	Corvina, Rondinella, and Molinara
Red	Barbera d'Asti	Piedmont	Barbera
Red	Chianti	Tuscany	Mostly Sangiovese
Red	Brunello di Montalcino	Tuscany	Brunello (a grape closely related to Sangiovese)
Red	Piave Merlot	Veneto	Merlot
Red	Morellino di Scansano	Tuscany	Mostly Sangiovese
Red	Taurasi	Campania	Aglianico and Piedirosso
Red	Salice Salentino	Puglia	Negro Amaro
White	Soave	Veneto	Garganega and Trebbiano
White	Gavi	Piedmont	Cortese
White	Orvieto	Umbria	Trebbiano, Verdello, and Grechetto
White	Greco di Tufo	Campania	Greco and Coda di Volpe

Germany

While Chardonnay-based wines are far more familiar to the American public, Rieslings, especially those from Germany, are just as good. When people think of German wines, they usually think of Riesling. But Germany has other wines of distinction as well.

German wine has not played a significant role in the United States wine boom, probably for a few different reasons.

First of all, Californian versions of Riesling haven't been so great. Because of this, Americans aren't inspired to "go to the source" as they have done for other grapes. Although many consumers who've been hooked by Californian Chardonnay experiment with the French Chardonnays of Burgundy, not so with German Rieslings.

Second, German wines have a reputation for being too sweet. Although many of Germany's wines are less dry than Americans prefer, Germany does make some wonderful dry Riesling. Liebfraumilch, an overrated and somewhat sweet wine, was briefly in vogue in the states in the late 1960s and early '70s. This wine is partly responsible for the misconception that German wine equals sweet wine.

When people look at the indecipherable German wine labels on today's wines, many wonder if they are looking at a Liebfraumilch-type wine. Perhaps if people understood the labels on the bottles, they would be more willing to experiment with German wines.

Following is a list to help you decipher those labels. Like the other European Union countries, Germany has a government-regulated wine-rating system. Of the three levels of quality, the top two are exported to the United States. The levels are:

- **Qualitätswein mit Prädikat (QmP):** This description is used for the highest quality wine.
- **Qualitätswein Bestimmter Anbaugebiete (QbA):** This is the designation for middle-quality wine.
- **Tafelwein:** This is the lowest-level wine.

QbA indicates quality wine from a quality region. Unless the label specifies that the wine is a Riesling, then it is made from another variety or, more likely, varieties. Other common German varieties are:

Sylvaner
Müller-Thurgau (a cross between Riesling and Sylvaner)
Gewürztraminer

Because QmP is the designation of highest quality, QmP wine labels offer more information about the wine. The Prädikats, or levels of distinction, indicate the sugar level at harvest. Because Germany's vineyards are so far north, it is difficult to get the grapes to ripen, hence grape sugars are highly prized. Chaptalization, the addition of sugars to increase the alcohol content via fermentation, is not allowed in QmP wines.

The Prädikats, or distinctions, are as follows:

- **Kabinett:** Normal, fully ripe grapes (9.5 percent minimum potential alcohol).
- **Spätlese:** "Late-harvested" grapes, which may produce slightly sweet wine.
- **Auslese:** Individually selected, very ripe bunches used to make sweet wine.
- **Beerenauslese:** Individually selected, very ripe grapes ("berries") used to make extremely sweet dessert wine.
- **Trockenbeerenauslese:** Individually selected, *botrytis*-afflicted grapes used to make the sweetest, most expensive German dessert wines.
- **Eiswein (icewine):** A relatively new Prädikat reserved for wines that are made from grapes naturally frozen on the vine and pressed while frozen. This method concentrates sugar, as much of the grape's water is left behind as ice crystals.

Look for the word *trocken* on your German wine label as well; this means dry. *Halbtrocken* means half-dry.

QmP Kabinett and Spätlese wines are as complex and delicious as Chardonnays in the $12 to $18 price range. A growing trend in German wine is varietal-labeled Riesling QbA wines. At $8 to $10, these wines represent a very good value and match well with Asian cuisine because their touch of sweetness puts out the spicy fire.

German Sparkling Wine

Germany enjoys a healthy sparkling-wine industry. German bubbly, known as Sekt, is quite different from French and Californian sparkling wines, which are usually made from Chardonnay and Pinot Noir. Sekt is produced from Riesling and other German varieties, and it can be of high quality when produced by the Champagne method.

Of the many wine-producing areas in Germany, the two most outstanding are the Mosel-Saar-Ruwer region (along the Mosel River and its two tributaries), and the three contiguous regions along the Rhine River:

Rheingau
Rheinhessen
Rheinpfalz

The Riesling grape is the top grape in both areas. Fine Mosel Riesling tends to have mineral and citrus notes, with the classic Riesling floral bouquet. Rhine Riesling is usually richer, with apricot-like fruit. These rival areas distinguish themselves by bottle color: bright green for Mosel wines, brown for Rhines.

Spain

Spain has a history of wine production as old as that of France, yet her wines are not nearly as well known to American consumers. With a hot and dry climate, Spain seems like the perfect place to bring grapes to full ripeness. However, the scientific and technological developments that have improved European winemaking over the centuries have had little influence on the Spanish wine industry until very recently. Modern Spanish winemaking is presently undergoing a quality boom, and a variety of affordable, world-class reds as well as a few interesting whites are joining sherry and inexpensive Spanish sparkling wine (Cava) on our store shelves.

As noted in Chapter 2, "Sherry" is the anglicized name of the southeastern Spanish city of Jerez de la Frontiera and has long been Spain's best and most famous wine. The white Palomino grape develops delicacy and finesse in the chalky soils of the legally defined Jerez district, even though the district's withering heat would make soup of most fine grape varieties. Unfortunately, the wine boom of the last three decades hasn't done much for sherry; if anything, newly converted wine enthusiasts tend to view sherry as a manufactured product quite distinct from fine wine, and port is most often their fortified wine of choice. (Also see Chapter 2 for a detailed explanation of sherry production.)

Rioja

The Rioja region in North-Central Spain was one of the few beneficiaries of *phylloxera* and other vineyard scourges of the 1800s. Many French winemakers and merchants became suddenly unemployed when the vineyards of France were struck down, first by mildew and later by *phylloxera*, and a number of them set up shop in the Rioja region right over the Pyrenees Mountains from Southern France. The red wines of Rioja, made from the Tempranillo and Garnacha (Grenache) varieties, were greatly improved by the Gallic influence and quickly gained favor in France.

Catalonia

Unlike many of Spain's wine regions, which roast in high summer temperatures and struggle for sufficient water (irrigation is forbidden in Spain), the region of Catalonia along the Mediterranean coast enjoys a climate moderated by its proximity to the sea. This is the seat of the gigantic Spanish sparkling wine industry, whose famous producers include the twin giants Freixenet and Codorniu. "Cava," as Spanish sparkling wine is known, is produced by the Champagne method from lesser known, native white grape varieties such as Macabeo and Xarel-lo. (The Champagne region's Chardonnay grape was only approved for Cava production in 1986.)

Priorato

The summer temperatures just a few miles inland from the Mediterranean coast are quite warm, and the Catalonian subregion of Priorato has all the makings of a first-rate (if tiny) wine district: relentless sun, stony soils nearly incapable of supporting other vegetation, and a renewed interest from modern winemakers, who use French barrels and have planted better-known red varieties such as Cabernet Sauvignon and Syrah to complement the indigenous Garnacha and Cariñena (the French Carignane). Some truly world-class red wines displaying both muscle and elegance have emerged from Priorato in recent years, and great things are expected of this region in the near future.

Ribero Duero

Important wine regions throughout the world are often distinguished by a river, and one of the world's great wine rivers rises in the
central Spanish highlands north of Madrid. Downstream, in Portugal,
it is known as the Douro, the home of the port industry, but in Spain
it is called the Duero. Along its upland banks, the Ribera del Duero
wine region is challenging the nearby Rioja area for supremacy among
Spanish wine regions. Although the Ribero del Duero region bakes in
merciless Spanish sunshine by day, cool nighttime temperatures associated with this location's high altitude keep acid levels in the grapes
at an acceptable level. Red wine from Ribero del Duero is produced
from the Tinto Fino grape, a close relative of the Tempranillo variety.

Noteworthy Whites from Spain

There are few Spanish dry white wines of importance. White
Rioja, made from the native Viura grape, can be pleasant for fans of
oaky flavors, and there is a growing amount of varietal Chardonnay
and other internationally marketable varieties being produced in the
Catalonian subregion of Penedés. Perhaps the most distinctive Spanish
white wine on the market today is varietal Albariño, produced near
the Atlantic coast to the north of Portugal. Due to its thick skins,
Albariño makes a heavy wine, often reminiscent of the Rhône's Viog-
niers. As such, it can be an interesting antidote to Chardonnay fatigue.

Portugal

Portugal is, perhaps, the last bastion of truly old-world winemaking.
Here, wine estates have thus far refused to uproot their native varieties

in order to stick Chardonnay and Merlot vines in the ground. There is a downside to this rare and admirable respect for past tradition, however. The world of Portuguese table wine is a maze of unrecognizable grape varieties and obscure place-names. Port, produced in the Douro valley, is the "winiest" of the world's fortified wines and is well known to American wine drinkers. (A full treatment of port is given in Chapter 2.) Perhaps the Portuguese table wines best known to American consumers are the twin rosés Mateus and Lancer's, which were wildly popular a few decades ago at the beginning of the wine boom.

Vinho Verde—"green wine"—is produced from native grape varieties and vinified in a distinctively food-friendly style—sharply dry and acidic, low in alcohol, and slightly fizzy. Portuguese reds, impenetrable as their labels may be, are often the best values around for fans of puckery dry, rustic wines under $10. Portugal is not without its expensive treasures, however. The most highly acclaimed Portuguese red table wines come from the Douro river valley and are made from the same grapes used for port production. The best of these Douro reds command prices similar to those of highly rated Californian reds.

Austria

Austrian wine is quite possibly the most underappreciated treasure in the world of wine today. Perhaps American wine consumers think of Austrian wine as sweet, or it is too easy to confuse Austria with Australia. Or maybe the wine drinkers of today remember the infamous Austrian wine scandal of two decades ago, when some Austrian Trockenbeerenauslese dessert wines were found to contain additives that made them seem thicker than usual. The truth is that the

Austrians forcefully responded to that scandal by enacting the most comprehensive (if difficult to understand) body of wine laws in the world, and Austrian wine is held to some of the highest standards in the world for purity, truthful labeling, and quality. Of course, none of this would matter if the wines were not of such high quality to begin with.

Separated from nearby Northern Italian wine regions by the imposing Alps, the vineyards of Eastern Austria, first cultivated by the wine-loving ancient Celts, are blessed with a typically continental climate—hot summer days, cool summer nights, and enough autumn warmth to bring quality wine grapes to full ripeness. In the southeast corner, in the foothills of the Alps, the Styria region produces only a small amount of Austria's wine, albeit of high quality. Chardonnay, known locally as "Morillon," grows in the steep Styrian hillside vineyards, as does Sauvignon Blanc. The Pinot Blanc grape, known locally as Weissburgunder, also performs well in Styria, and so does the red Zweigelt grape, a popular crossing of the alpine red variety St. Laurent with the German Blaufränkisch. To the north of Styria, along the Hungarian border, the Burgenland region partially surrounds Lake Neusiedlersee and yields some of the world's greatest dessert wines as well as Austria's boldest reds. However, most of the country's top-quality wines are produced in the northeast corner of Austria, in "Lower Austria," situated along the Danube.

Like the other wine-producing districts of Lower Austria, the Weinviertel produces much of its wine from Austria's own white variety, the Grüner Veltliner grape. And yet a wide variety of other grapes are grown in the sprawling Weinviertel district, including Chardonnay, Riesling, Weissburgunder, and Sauvignon Blanc among whites, and Zweigelt and even Cabernet Sauvignon among reds. Although the Weinviertel's reputation has long been based on quantity rather than quality, the wines of the district are rapidly improving in the hands of a new generation of winemakers. Farther up the Danube River Valley, the districts of Kremstal, Kamtal, and Wachau also produce delicious (if pricier) Grüner Veltliners and brilliant, bone-dry Rieslings, the best of which are among the finest dry white wines in the world.

The United States

Much of the early history of American wine involved a struggle for superiority between the colonial agriculturalists in the East and the relatively recent settlers in California. Although the Eastern states held the early lead, California's supremacy as an American wine-producing region has been unquestionable since the late 1800s. Although wine is now produced in all fifty states, few states besides California successfully produce quality wine on a noteworthy scale. In fact, only Oregon, Washington, and New York produce wines that are consumed beyond their own borders in commercially significant quantities. Many of the wineries in the other states rely heavily on tourist traffic and the accompanying retail wine sales at the winery's door.

California

The sunny hillsides and valleys of Central and Northern California have proved to be ideal locations for bringing *vinifera* varieties—even stubborn ripeners like Cabernet Sauvignon—to lush, full ripeness. This is possible because of California's long, dry, and hot summers.

Shortly after prohibition was repealed, two Californian academics at the University of California at Davis, professors Maynard Amerine and Albert Winkler, devised an ingenious method for classifying Californian wine regions according to their capacity for heat accumulation. The Amerine-Winkler scale is based on the average monthly temperature above 50° during the growing season from April through October. A "degree-day" is a day with a 24-hour average temperature of 51°, and, therefore, a single day with an average temperature of 75° would contribute 25 degree-days to the heat accumulation required for ripening grapes. Amerine and Winkler classified the established wine regions of California in order of increasing heat accumulation, expressed in degree-days:

- **Region I:** Fewer than 2,500 degree-days
- **Region II:** 2,500–3,000
- **Region III:** 3,000–3,500
- **Region IV:** 3,500–4,000
- **Region V:** More than 4,000 degree-days

It is generally true in California as well as the rest of the world that greater heat accumulation makes possible larger crops of grapes. However, as the Romans and French learned, often the finest wines come from cooler vineyard sites where the warmth is spread over a longer ripening period, and grapes must struggle somewhat to achieve full ripeness. And so the finest dry table wines of California are usually produced in the regions I and II, such as the cooler parts of the Napa and Sonoma Valleys, while the hotter regions, like the vast San Joaquin Valley, are better suited to the production of fortified wines, raisins, and table grapes. It follows that there is an ideal balance for a vineyard location: warm enough to bring the grapes to full ripeness at economically rewarding crop levels, yet cool enough to prolong this ripening period in order to allow maximum flavor development. California, particularly Napa Valley, has many such sites.

Napa Valley and Sonoma Valley

Napa Valley has long enjoyed primacy among the wine regions of California, although the others are rapidly closing the gap. Stretching twenty miles north from San Francisco Bay, Napa Valley is characterized by a hot valley floor, cooler hillsides and mountaintops, and world-class Cabernet Sauvignon. Napa Chardonnay is also a star, and Napa versions of heat-loving, old-vine Zinfandel and Petite Sirah can be excellent. Unfortunately, the Napa region has evolved into a Mecca of spas, resorts, and mansions, and the skyrocketing real estate prices in Napa Valley have helped to drive up wine prices.

Sonoma Valley, meanwhile, has lagged behind Napa Valley in both wine accolades and gentrification. While Sonoma certainly turns out its share of quality Cabernet Sauvignon, the cooler coastal areas of Sonoma have proved to be a reliable source of some of the state's finest Chardonnay. These Sonoma subregions are also noteworthy for their Pinot Noir, a noble variety that fails to thrive in Napa Valley's warmth. Likewise, the Carneros district—the southernmost tip of both Napa and Sonoma Counties—is a perfect venue for Pinot Noir and other heat-shy grapes.

The Central Coast

The Santa Cruz mountain area south of San Francisco Bay was the cradle of nineteenth-century fine wine production in California. In this area, Paul Masson and Charles LeFranc cultivated newly imported, premium grape varieties from France. Today the vast "Central Coast" region of central California, stretching from the Santa Cruz mountains south to Santa Barbara, is rapidly becoming known for a wide variety of fine wines, from Chardonnay and Pinot Noir in the coastal draws and on mountaintops, to Zinfandel and Cabernet Sauvignon in Paso Robles. Rhône varieties such as Syrah, Grenache, and Viognier are also grown in several subregions by the innovative "Rhône Rangers."

The Pacific Northwest

The Pacific Northwest may actually be on equal footing with California in certain aspects of wine production. While any overview of wine production in the United States must focus on California, the wines of the Pacific Northwest cannot be ignored. California is among the finest wine regions in the world—a region that produces more high-quality wine than most wine-producing *countries*. However, not all grape varieties thrive in its warmth, and the Pacific Northwest with its cooler growing areas complements California perfectly. Quality wines from popular grape varieties come from Oregon and Washington. Although these states combined produce far less wine than the state of California, the Pacific Northwest actually enjoys some advantages over California when it comes to production.

One factor is rooted in economics. The wine boom has driven the price of California vineyard acreage sky-high, which, in turn, has inflated production costs. This is why Washington State Merlot is often the equal of similarly priced Californian versions. Another factor is the climate. Although the Californian sun ripens grapes with ease, the Yakima and Columbia Valleys of Washington, while somewhat cooler than California's Napa and Sonoma Valleys, enjoy more hours of summer sunshine because of their more northerly latitude. The relentless warmth and sunshine in California's Napa Valley might be perfect for Cabernet Sauvignon, but other premium red varieties—namely Merlot and Syrah—require a little less heat accumulation to ripen properly. Cooler temperatures allow these earlier-ripening red grape varieties to ripen at an optimum pace and develop full, complex flavors, while the longer hours of sunshine provide them sufficient heat accumulation. Cabernet Sauvignon, meanwhile, also performs well in this Washington State climate, but with less power and more finesse than its Napa Valley counterparts.

While California certainly produces enough Chardonnay to go around, there are many fine Washington State versions of this ubiquitous variety from the Pacific Northwest. Washington State also excels in the production of Riesling, a cool climate variety that doesn't perform so well in California's high temperatures. If the Washington State wine regions are on par with California's—in quality, if not quantity—it can be said that the cool vineyards of Oregon have some definite advantages over California's warm valleys.

California winemakers, so successful with heat-loving Cabernet Sauvignon, struggled for many decades with their Pinot Noirs before finally seeking cooler terrain. In the early 1960s, pioneering winemaker David Lett and others recognized the Pinot Noir's affinity for the cool and cloudy climate in Oregon's Willamette Valley. Today, Oregon Pinot Noirs are often described as "Burgundian"—a tasting note rarely associated with the often-overripe Californian versions. Perhaps the highest compliment ever paid to Oregon Pinot Noir comes from the venerable Burgundy wine producer Joseph Drouhin. The Drouhin family considered Oregon Pinot Noir to be of such high quality—especially after they watched Oregon wines defeat their own in a blind tasting—that they purchased vineyard land in the Willamette Valley and started producing their own Oregon Pinot Noir. Today, Domaine Drouhin "Cuvee Laurene" is considered to be among the finest American Pinot Noirs.

Pinot Gris is the other success story in Oregon. This grape variety, also grown in Alsace and Italy, grows best in a cool climate such as Oregon's. California winemakers have yet to click with this variety, but Oregon Pinot Gris at its best is comparable to the fine versions from Alsace, France.

New York

New York State, another cool-climate wine region, was once a major wine-producing state. In recent years, this region has redefined itself. The Finger Lakes district, established in the 1860s, was based on the production of wine from native North American grape varieties and native/French hybrids, vineyard stock capable of withstanding the brutal Northeastern winters. It was only a matter of time, however, before the new railroads enabled the Californian wine industry to overtake the wineries of the Eastern states, and New York's domestic market steadily dwindled.

Then, in the 1950s, Dr. Konstantin Frank, a Russian-born German who immigrated to the United States after World War II, began successfully planting *vinifera* varieties in the Finger Lakes region. His success with Chardonnay, Gewürztraminer, and especially Riesling encouraged other widespread plantings. Today, the Finger Lakes region is enjoying a rebirth. There are suddenly dozens of small, hands-on producers—no doubt the beneficiaries of retail sales at their wineries—who produce excellent and affordable Rieslings that are drier and more full-bodied than their German cousins.

The New York State fine wine industry is not confined to the Finger Lakes. Winemakers on the north fork of Long Island, an area long known as an agricultural Eden but only under vines since 1973, have demonstrated that high-quality, Bordeaux-style Merlot can be produced in this area's sandy soils and mild climate. Although several Long Island wines have earned recognition from wine critics, whether or not Long Island's wineries can survive solely on the merits of their wine, rather than tourist traffic, remains to be seen. It's too early to tell.

Argentina

As a wine-producing (and wine-loving) nation, Argentina enjoys many natural assets beneficial to wine production. Her vineyard regions are located in the western part of the country, scattered along the eastern foothills of the Andes range. These towering mountains shield the Argentine vineyards from Pacific rainstorms and yet provide them with a steady flow of water from their melting icecaps. Furthermore, the low humidity in this near-desert region prevents molds and other vineyard problems. Although it would be possible to cultivate a wide range of grape varieties in these conditions, it seems that the Argentine wine industry has adopted the Malbec grape variety of Southwest France as its own.

Brought to Argentina from France a century ago, the Malbec grape fares far better in Argentina's dry conditions than it ever did in its native Bordeaux, where it was especially susceptible to the mildew and rot encouraged by maritime humidity. In the hands of a great producer, Argentine Malbec is fruity and lush with a moderate backbone of tannin and acidity. Dr. Nicolas Catena, proprietor of the Botega Catena Zapata winery in Mendoza, produces some of the finest (and most expensive) versions of Argentine Malbec.

Other grape varieties that perform well or show future promise in Argentina are the usual international varieties Cabernet Sauvignon, Merlot, and Chardonnay. As in many other fine wine regions of the world, the Syrah grape is becoming significant in Argentina. However, if you want to try something a little farther from the mainstream, look for Argentine wine made from the Criolla grape, a low-end *vinifera* variety brought to Argentina hundreds of years ago. It is still quite popular in Argentina as an inexpensive, heavyweight white.

Chile

Chile, the 3,000-mile-long nation along the Pacific Coast of South America, is rapidly becoming one of the most important sources of inexpensive varietal wines in the world. California wines have steadily increased in price, to the point that a varietally correct $15 bottle of California Merlot or Cabernet Sauvignon is headed for the endangered species list. Chile is benefiting from this increase in Californian wine prices, producing generous quantities of California-style wines with forward and obvious fruit flavors.

Chile's wine regions are located in the approximate center of the country, just south of the capital city of Santiago, about halfway between the Pacific Ocean and the rugged Andes mountains. Traveling south from Santiago, the region names most likely to appear on a wine label are:

Casablanca   Rapel
Maipo   Colchagua

However, like most New-World wines, Chilean wine is generally labeled primarily by grape variety. For the most part, the varieties echo those produced in neighboring Argentina, with one significant exception.

The Carmènere variety was once cultivated extensively in Bordeaux, until it was overshadowed by other varieties and faded from use. At some point, it was brought to Chile and misidentified as Merlot. Until recently, it was labeled as such. Under close scrutiny by ampelographers (grapevine scientists), the Carmènere grape was reidentified as distinct from Merlot, and many Chilean wineries now proudly bottle varietal Carmènere.

Chile has a reputation as a source of inexpensive varietal wine, mostly reds. In order to establish itself as a source of fine wine, however, Chile must overcome this reputation. There has been a strong push toward quality winemaking in recent years, driven by significant investment from European and American wine producers. It remains to be seen if the American wine consumer will accept higher priced, premium versions of Chilean wine.

South Africa

Fine wine has been produced in South Africa since the 1600s, when the region was colonized by the Dutch. However, because of the white South African government's policy of racial apartheid, South Africa was politically and economically ostracized for several decades during the wine boom and thus unable to reap its benefits. Although today it is politically acceptable to support the South African industry, there has not been any wholesale shift in consumer interest toward South African wine following its entry into the American market. This will undoubtedly change, because the wines of South Africa are rapidly improving.

Almost all of South Africa's vineyards are concentrated near the continent's southern tip, where the Indian Ocean meets the Atlantic. A cool current of Antarctic air and water refreshes the region with temperatures chillier than its warm latitude might suggest. Even so, until recently most of South Africa's vineyards were planted in plains just a little too warm for fine wine production. Furthermore, many of the South African vineyard sites are in acidic soils that require costly amelioration. However, even with such disadvantages, there are some excellent South African wines on the market.

Pinotage is a red grape variety nearly unique to its South African birthplace. Also known by the name Hermitage, Pinotage is an attempted cross of Pinot Noir and Syrah. However, some vines got mixed up, and the Cinsault of Southern France—far more pedestrian a grape than the intended Syrah—was successfully crossed with Pinot Noir instead. This new variety has been a success in South Africa, so much so that it has encouraged a few Californian vinters to give it a try. There have also been numerous successes with Cabernet Sauvignon, Merlot, and Syrah, known in South Africa as Shiraz.

Chenin Blanc (known in South Africa as "Steen") and Chardonnay grapes do well in this country, as does Sauvignon Blanc. The best of these wines are light and crisp, with contrasting elements of fruit and minerals.

The South African system of wine labeling requires that the geographic region of origin be specified on the wine labels. The most notable regions are:

Swartland
Stellenbosch
Paarl

As with American wines, South African wines must be comprised of at least 75 percent of a single grape variety in order to qualify for varietal labeling.

Australia

Australia has been making wine since soon after the first shipload of British settlers (and prisoners) arrived in 1788. Geographically isolated from the rest of the wine-producing world, Australia developed her own sophisticated winemaking technology largely independent of the techniques developed in Europe. This factor, along with a combination of intense sunshine and cool breezes, helps to make Australian wines unique.

If California's famous wine regions are best characterized by their capacity for heat accumulation, Australia's regions are even more so. The sun-baked interior of Australia boasts only one brave wine producer; the rest of the Australian producers bask in the sun of more hospitable and grape-friendly regions clustered in the three southeastern states and one small area in the southwestern corner, in the state of Western Australia. Unlike almost all other wine regions on Earth, ripeness is never an issue in the vineyards of Australia, where the relentless sunshine reliably brings even high yields of grapes to absolute ripeness.

The hot and humid Hunter Valley, historically a source of Semillon and Chardonnay, is close to the eastern coast, just north of Sydney in the state of New South Wales. It is perhaps the Hunter Valley's proximity to Sydney, as much as the quality of its wines, that has brought the region such renown.

The Southeast . . .

Farther down the coast, the state of Victoria is a source of unusual dessert wines. The sweet Muscat and Tokay-based dessert wines of Rutherglen—known as "stickies" Down Under—are fortified blends of sweet wines from multiple vintages going back several decades. Elsewhere in Victoria is the cool Yarra Valley region, a rare source of Australian Pinot Noir, and the historic Great Western region.

The state of South Australia, perhaps Australia's most important wine-producing state, is home to several great wine regions. The Clare and Barossa Valleys are both famous for their Shiraz (Syrah)–based reds and, thanks to a strong German heritage in the state, dry Rieslings characterized by the uniquely Australian hint of lime favor. The Padthaway region is a source of high quality and affordable Chardonnay, and the very Australian-sounding Coonawarra region is considered Australia's finest source of Cabernet Sauvignon.

. . . And the Southwest

Thousands of miles away, on Western Australia's Indian Ocean coast, the small but rapidly improving Margaret River region is producing Cabernet Sauvignons and Chardonnays that compete with the finest wines of Australia's southeastern wineries.

Market Consolidation

Because of a relatively recent flurry of mergers and acquisitions, the future of Australian wine seems to be in the hands of a few gigantic companies. The Wolf Blass winery, for instance, is now part of the conglomerate **Beringer-Blass Wine Estates** and includes numerous, high-profile Californian wineries and other Australian wineries such as The Rothbury Estate and Jamieson's Run. The wine group **Southcorp** is a giant in the Australian wine industry whose properties include Penfold's, Rosemount, and Lindemans. Meanwhile, Hardy's is now part of **Constellation Brands**, which has recently become, through various mergers, the world's largest wine company. What effect these recent changes will have on Australian wine remains to be seen. There are still a few small, quality-oriented "boutique" producers whose wines are generally available to connoisseurs.

New Zealand

The Southern Pacific nation of New Zealand, comprised of two main islands, has long been famous for her lamb wool, a world-class rugby team, and miles of unspoiled trout rivers. However, in the past decade, New Zealand has also become synonymous with distinctive and affordable wines made from the Sauvignon Blanc grape, a noble white variety that, even in its most brilliant manifestations, has never generated much excitement among the wine-buying public. Although it is not the most widely planted grape variety in New Zealand (that distinction belongs to Chardonnay), the Sauvignon Blanc grape appears to have found an ideal setting in New Zealand, particularly in the cool Marlborough region on the South Island. In the hands of skilled winemakers, Marlborough Sauvignon Blanc delivers an array of varietally correct aromas, ranging from grapefruit and gooseberry to funky, animal scents. These aromas are accompanied by a racy acidic profile that makes this wine especially delicious to enjoy with dinner, rather than to drink by itself during cocktails.

Don't Quit Your Day Job!

Now that the New Zealand wine industry has found its niche, it is fair to ask: Is New Zealand capable of generating similar successes with other grape varieties, or will the New Zealand wine industry stick to the grape variety that, against all odds, has brought it to prominence? The Kiwis keep promising the wine world that an equally attractive Pinot Noir will soon follow their Sauvignon Blanc. So far, try as they might, the few successful New Zealand versions of this most difficult of grapes have been overshadowed by a great many more failures. The warmer North Island, meanwhile, promises Bordeaux-like Cabernet Sauvignon and Merlot, but these remain to be seen. Suffice it to say that a heretofore unheralded and unproven wine region that has succeeded in putting Sauvignon Blanc on every wine lover's map has much to be thankful for, and would do well to further develop its proven assets before trying to broaden its offerings.

The Rest of the World

This list of wine-producing countries is by no means comprehensive. There are well-made wines from many other regions that are beyond the scope of this book. If you're feeling adventurous, ask your local wine merchant about fine wines from Eastern Europe, or even Canada.

Part 4

Choosing and Serving Wine

Chapter 10

The Economics of Wine

JUST AS WITH ANY OTHER product on the market today, the price of wine to consumers is determined by several different factors; competition, supply and demand, government regulation, and the cost of production all play a role. Here is an inside look at the economics of wine.

Economics 101

Picture Main Street, USA, filled with nothing but wine and liquor stores, standing shoulder-to-shoulder for many blocks, each stocked with every known brand on Earth. This fictitious situation would most certainly lead to a degree of competition (called *perfect competition* in econo-speak), such that a consumer could conveniently move from one store to another, shopping for the best price on a particular alcoholic beverage. This state of affairs would, in turn, lead to *perfect price elasticity of demand*, meaning that the profits on such items would be razor-thin because any storekeeper who dared to charge the slightest bit more than the others would immediately lose all of his business to his neighbors.

Although this arrangement might be nice for the consumer (until most stores went broke and the survivors then raised their prices), the fact is that local and state governments have good reason to limit the number of stores in a given town or city, and they do so. In the hypothetical situation above, it's perfectly easy to walk next door to the next liquor store to get a better price. In the real world, however, because the number of liquor stores is limited in a given area, it's not so simple.

Since the hassle of driving across town and parking all over again somewhere else might not be worth the dollar saved, the demand for the desired product becomes somewhat *inelastic*. In other words, demand doesn't significantly diminish because of a noticeably higher price. This way, the government manages to control the supply of alcoholic beverages more effectively and simultaneously keep the prices high enough for a few retail license holders to make a reasonable profit. And if retailers are making a profit, they can be more easily regulated in a manner that contributes to the public safety and welfare.

Wine Merchants in the Real World

In reality, Main Street, USA, has far fewer wine and liquor stores, but it is still easy to compare prices via advertisements on mass-produced and widely distributed national brands such as Budweiser beer and Stolichnaya vodka. Consequently, the markups on those types of items remain rather small. This is not so with wine, however.

There are thousands of wine producers in the world, and while "Bud" and "Stoli" drinkers are usually quite loyal to their favorite brand, wine buyers, who have so many choices, are generally more prone to hop from one label to another. Therefore, if a store is out of one Chardonnay that sells for, say, $9.99, the wine manager might easily recommend a perfectly satisfying alternative at a similar price . . . And yet, every wine is unique (unique in terms of *terroir*, vintage, and so on). This aura of uniqueness is known as *product differentiation* and, by obscuring direct comparisons between similarly priced wines, it further prevents *perfect competition* in the wine market.

The result? Greater profit margins at the retail level on wine than on either beer or liquor. The exception to this is the relatively small set of wines that have achieved "brand status." Well-known and widely distributed household names such as Kendall-Jackson Chardonnay and Ravenswood Zinfandel are more subject to price comparison from one store to another than are lesser-known wines, and, therefore, they usually make less money per bottle for the retailer than lesser-known labels. However, because these wines got to be "brands" in the first place due to strong customer demand, they are usually fast-moving items that earn their floor space with high-volume sales. Now that we know that the retailer charges a much higher markup on wine (40 to 50 percent over wholesale cost) than on beer or liquor, let's follow the money trail all the way back to the vines.

Supply Side Economics . . .

Where do stores get their wine? Most states have a three-tiered distribution system in place that brings wine from the winery (or its designated agent) to an in-state wholesaler who sells it to the store where you then purchase it. So a bottle of wine that sells for $15 retail probably cost the store $10 to buy from the wholesaler, and the wholesaler $7.50 to buy from the winery. It might seem tempting to try to bypass this gauntlet and save a few bucks, but the alcohol business is a maze of regulations that makes these sorts of shortcuts very difficult.

We consumers are limited to wines that have come through this three-tiered system, which, as we see, doubles the cost of wine for us. Not bad, considering what is done to us on many other products we buy, such as clothing and furniture. Now, how much does it cost the winery to make a bottle of your favorite wine? Let's look at the supply side of the equation.

The Cost of Doing Business

Wine costs money to produce, and one fundamental cost of winemaking worth considering before anything else is the cost of land use, be it rent, mortgage, or alternative use. (If you choose to grow grapes rather than sell the land to a developer for a million dollars, the opportunity cost of owning the vineyard is quite high.) If the vineyard land is relatively expensive, it is obviously desirable to produce similarly expensive wine there in order to better offset the land cost; this would explain why only pricey wines are produced in the dear soil of the Napa Valley.

Although basic wine made from grapes grown on inexpensive land is cheaper to produce than milk, wineries have to shell out plenty of money on lots of different things in order to make good, really good, or great wine. For starters, state-of-the-art equipment, new French oak barrels, and top-quality fruit add to the cost of winemaking. New French oak cooperage, for instance, adds about $2.50 to the cost of each bottle, and top-quality fruit is often the result of literally throwing away as much as half the crop during the summer so that the remaining fruit becomes that much riper and richer. As previously discussed, these sorts of expenses often fuel a self-fulfilling prophesy: The wine-buying public expects high quality (and prices) from renowned wine producers, who in turn spare no expense in annually turning out an exquisite and accordingly costly product to their eager and established market. Finally, the costs of producing wine are related to the size of the winery. A tiny, 5,000-case-per-year operation might have some of the same fixed costs as a winery twice its size, and thus the larger winery would enjoy *economies of scale* that enable it to bottle wine at a lower cost per bottle than the smaller winery can.

. . . And Demand

Next, let's look at the demand side of things. A basic assumption in our semi-free-enterprise economy is that wine is fairly priced. (We trust that competition keeps it that way.) As such, it may be tempting to generalize that all wines retailing for, say, $9.99 are of equal quality and value and that one's preference of one wine over another is simply a matter of personal taste. Now, supposing that this gross overgeneralization were true, how would you choose a wine at that price?

The consumer's expectations regarding a particular bottle of wine might be the result of many different factors: previous experience, advertising, a trusted recommendation, a wine magazine rating, or even a pretty label. Of course, all $9.99 wines are not of equal quality . . . nor are equally priced cars, homes, or professional athletes. There are bargains to be found in the wine store, wines with very high quality-to-price ratios (QPRs). The reasons for such inequities are many: International currency fluctuations and good old-fashioned supply and demand are two, for starters. It's your local wine merchant's job to find good values for you. You might also search for them yourself by perusing reputable wine reviews and calculating QPRs on your own—just divide the reviewer's score by the retail price. (For example, refer to wine reviews on *Wine Spectator* magazine's Web site, at *www.winespectator.com*.)

More Economic Theory

A few other notions from the realm of microeconomics are relevant to this discussion. The concept of *diminishing marginal utility* explains the decrease in the pleasure obtained from further consumption. If we apply this concept to quality rather than quantity, then consumers would have an upper price limit, a price above which they would be averse to paying for more quality. (For example, while a consumer might consider the jump in quality from a $10 bottle to a $20 bottle to be well worth the money, she might not be willing to pay for the difference between a $30 and a $40 bottle and would rather spend *that* $10 on other things.)

Finally, your wine of choice might have *cachet value* (which often increases the price) above and beyond its *intrinsic value*. For instance, while a distinguished dinner guest from Argentina might be moved to tears when you serve him the legendary Catena Alta from his homeland, he might not enjoy it quite as much if he doesn't actually know what he is drinking. Cachet value might well be defined as "how much you like the wine while reading its label" minus "how much you like the wine tasting it blind."

Restaurant Wine

The economics of restaurant wine pricing are somewhat different from those in the retail world. Many restaurants simply multiply the wholesale cost of each wine on the list by a factor of as much as three in order to arrive at the wine-list price. This formula would price all wines on the list at double the going retail price (assuming the 50 percent retail markup). A more sensible policy used by a growing number of establishments is to price wines on a sliding scale that marks up wines by a decreasing percentage as one moves up the price ladder: Thus, the $20 retail wine might still be priced at $40 on such a list, but a $60 retail wine would, perhaps, sell for $80, not $120. This encourages the customers to move up to better wines now and then by offering them better value (QPR) on high-end wines as an incentive to "trade up."

Wine by the glass in restaurants is rarely a bargain because that pricing tends to coincide with that of the martini program rather than the rest of the wine program. Don't be shocked to see a glass of wine in a swank restaurant offered for nearly the retail price of an entire 750ml bottle—it's not uncommon.

So is restaurant pricing on wine unfair? Not really, when you consider that a well-run restaurant usually earns at least as healthy a profit on the food, and you're paying for the ambience and service as well as the wine itself. In exchange for the additional money you pay for wine in restaurants, you are entitled to knowledgeable, prompt, and courteous service, clean and appropriate stemware, and wine at the proper serving temperature.

For more detailed information on restaurant wine pricing, see Chapter 12, Navigating the Restaurant Wine List.

Chapter 11

Shopping for Wine

UNLESS YOU SET OUT for the wine store with a specific bottle of wine in mind, you will have to make a buying decision based on limited information. Your goal is to bring home a wine you will like, at a price that's comfortable for you. In the end, you might end up with a bottle you've had in the past just because the choice was familiar and it was the most informed selection you could make. If you're looking to build your wine repertoire and branch out into new areas, you have to know how to shop around and navigate different types of wine stores.

A Guide to Wine Stores

Although every wine store is unique, it is possible to make some useful generalizations that might help you to decide where you should shop. First of all, the size of the store you're shopping in makes a difference. There are big stores; there are little stores; and there are stores in between. In most states, the big store can take advantage of its superior buying power and buy wine at a significant discount based on quantity. The bigger the store or chain, the bigger the discounts it is likely to receive. However, this doesn't necessarily mean that big stores are better for all of the people all of the time.

The second factor is expertise. Wine experts cost more money to employ than unskilled stock clerks. Therefore, the greater the degree of expertise in a store, the higher the labor cost. Wine stores (of any size) with excellent service generally cannot afford to offer much of their stock at rock-bottom prices.

So we have two variables at work here: size and expertise. In spite of the individual differences, we can get some sense of the retail wine-buying experience from these four hypothetical store types:

1. Small store with expertise
2. Small store without expertise
3. Big store with expertise
4. Big store without expertise

Small Store with Expertise

This store might well be a hobby, or at least a labor of love, for a semi-retired big shot from the wine industry or for a corporate fast-track dropout. Chances are that there won't be a bad bottle of wine in the store. The proprietor has probably tasted and personally selected them all. If you need advice or you're looking for a story about the vineyard, this is the best place to get it. Stores like this do well in college towns, because professors are naturally drawn to sources of information and expertise.

How to Tell if a Bottle of Wine Is in Good Shape

When you buy a bottle of wine, you don't want to buy damaged goods. Since there are no tires to kick, you need to use other tests.

1. Is the bottle filled up? This used to be more of an issue in the less industrial days of wine bottling. Check to see how high the wine is in the neck of that bottle compared to other bottles. There is no need to pay the same price for less wine.
2. Feel the cork through the wrapper on the top of the bottle. The cork shouldn't feel pushed in or out. The top of the cork should be close to flush with the top of the bottle. Cork movement can be indicative of a bad cork or a wine that has been exposed to temperature extremes.
3. Hold the bottle up to the light. Is it clear or murky? Sediment is only okay in an older bottle of wine. Wine from the same "batch" should be the same color. If you can't figure out which color is the right color, buy a different wine.

Before you buy wine at any store, you should be convinced that the store is kept at cool temperatures twenty-four hours a day. You also don't want to buy wines that are stored in places where they get a lot of light or are exposed to a radiator.

The downside to this type of store is that a staple item such as Kendall-Jackson Chardonnay will be far more expensive here than anyplace else. This boutique has far less purchasing power than the big stores and doesn't make it on volume.

Small Store Without Expertise

The wines in stores like this are often limited to huge brands such as Gallo, Fetzer, Kendall-Jackson, and the like. And why not? With all the money those sorts of wineries invest in advertising, plus their brand-name recognition, these wines sell themselves. The prices aren't cheap, but they might be cheap for a store this size. The selection is usually going to be disappointing at such a store.

However, some of these stores might have had some expertise at one time. Sometimes such expertise is asked to leave in order to keep the store from going bankrupt, because its excellent and costly wine inventory doesn't move fast enough. This means you might find a bargain that's a real treasure buried in the closeout bin, because the remaining staff did not know enough to mark it up as it aged. Browse this type of store very carefully the first time you go there.

In states where wine may be sold in food stores, the small store without expertise might be a convenience store. Here you are just looking for something you know is drinkable. Even mass-produced, brand-name wines seem to develop considerable complexity and finesse when purchased in the middle of nowhere five minutes before closing time.

Big Store with Expertise

At first glance, this type of store might look like a discount store, since the twenty-case floor stacks demonstrate evidence of considerable purchasing power. Upon further inspection, though, you see a lot of wines from remote or lesser-appreciated regions of the world—perhaps Argentina or Portugal. There might also be a small army of neatly dressed clerks assisting customers and offering expertise. Here you have a high labor cost, and at least part of the inventory isn't jumping off the shelves.

This big store with expertise is a good place to find wines that you can't find anywhere else, such as:

- Older wines, particularly red Bordeaux and Port.
- Hard-to-find Champagne, such as Blanc de Noirs or Brut Rosé.
- A good selection of Alsace and German wines.
- Wines from countries that don't export much wine.
- A highly allocated (i.e., very limited) wine.
- The perfect gift for a knowledgeable wine buff.

Big Store Without Expertise

These stores have truly strong purchasing power, not unlike the increasingly common "wholesale clubs" (many of which now sell wine). They buy single brands of liquor (or similarly popular wine) by the trailer load, and their wholesale suppliers jump whenever anyone from these stores calls to place an order. Gigantic stores can buy for less and can afford a lower markup on their inventory (25 to 40 percent over cost, rather than 50 to 60 percent) than small, "boutique" stores because of the volume of business they do. Some of the wines at these sorts of stores sell at prices below what the smaller stores pay wholesale for the same wines. The wine-buying public flocks to these stores to take advantage of the great prices and good selection.

Big stores without expertise might not have as esoteric a selection as the big stores with expertise, but if you are looking for popular wine driven by national advertising dollars (such as Moët et Chandon White Star Champagne; Kendall-Jackson Chardonnay; Meridian Chardonnay; Georges Duboeuf Beaujolais-Villages; Fetzer varietal wines; and Glen Ellen varietal wines) this is where you should be going, especially if you are going to be buying by the case.

Anatomy of a Wine Store

Now that you know a little bit about the various types of wine stores, you should be able to size up the stores in your area and know when to shop where. Now it's time for a tour of the typical wine store. With the exception of smaller stores, most wine shops often have a similar layout.

Big Bottles

The jug wall is a selection of easy-to-reach, inexpensive jug wines, usually near the entrance. The Californians are all there—Gallo, Inglenook, Almaden—with the old names: Burgundy, Chablis, and so on. These wines might take up quite a bit of the store's space because they still sell well, and the bottles are big, holding up to 4 liters. The small stores with expertise aren't likely to carry these wines because they avoid head-to-head price comparisons with bigger stores—known in the business as "getting beat up" on the price. Continuing along the wall near the California jug wines, you will perhaps see imported jug wines and the lesser fighting varietals. These two types are usually sold in the 1.5-liter bottle, and, like California jug wines, they enjoy brisk sales. This is a significant profit center for many liquor stores.

Fine Wines

The middle of the floor in a typical wine store is often filled with racks of 750ml bottles stored on their sides in metal or wooden racks. These wines are typically arranged by country, then maybe by region (depending on the country and size of the store), color, and variety. "Floor stacks" or "end caps" usually occupy the ends of these racks. Here you'll find popular wines bought and sold by the store in high volume. These wines can be terrific bargains if they are "rock-and-roll items"—major brands that sell so fast the store can afford to mark them up less. In a large store without expertise, a rock-and-roll item such as a well-known Chardonnay might be offered for only pennies over cost in order to attract customers into the store.

End caps can also serve an opposite purpose. The store might have bought the wine at a deep discount and then marked it up as much as 80 percent over their cost, bringing it back to the standard retail price. For obvious reasons, the store wants to sell a lot of this profitable brand. In either case, the wines sold on end caps are the wines the store wants you to buy, which is not surprising, since they are displayed in a way that makes them readily accessible to customers.

Wine Distribution in Retail Stores

When Prohibition was repealed in 1933, control of the actual distribution of alcoholic beverages was delegated to the individual states, which explains why alcohol laws vary so maddeningly from state to state. Most states—but not all—have what is known as a "three tier system," a distribution network in which state-licensed wholesalers purchase alcoholic beverages directly from their producers and then sell them to retail stores and restaurants, who in turn sell them to the public. (More on this in Chapter 10, The Economics of Wine.)

In several states the alcoholic beverage business is controlled to at least some degree by the state government and is highly regulated. Even in states in which the alcohol business is operated by the private sector, it is usually regulated in such a way that direct price competition between wholesalers is discouraged, which ultimately keeps retail prices from dropping as low as they might in a free market economy.

Why Don't Stores Carry Older Vintages?

If you want to shop for a rare old vintage of a special wine, you will probably have a hard time finding it. Retail stores have little economic incentive to carry older vintages of ageworthy wines, because the young wines that don't stay in the store for very long are the ones that pay the bills.

Stores may usually purchase wine from wholesalers with credit terms, which means that, in theory, stores are able to sell wine before they actually have to pay for it. If stores could do this with all of their wines, they would be extremely profitable; in reality, however, a store must offer a wide array of wines, some that turn over very quickly and other, usually more expensive wines that turn over more slowly. The wines that turn over quickly—before they are paid for, ideally— usually produce the most profits over the course of the year, and thus it is simply not worth it in most cases for retailers to buy new releases of ageworthy wines and hold them for several years while they slowly appreciate in value.

Volume Discounts

In some (but not all) states, retail wine stores get significant discounts when buying wine in large quantities. If retail stores can buy in significant quantity and pay less, why shouldn't you? Most retail wine stores offer 10 to 15 percent discounts for customers who buy mixed cases (12 assorted bottles of wine) and 15 to 20 percent for solid cases (12 bottles of the same wine). If you like a particular wine enough to drink it on a regular basis, buying it by the case makes much more sense than paying full price every time you want a bottle.

In the Know

Now that you know your way around the wine store and you understand how wine is distributed, it's time for you to choose a wine.

Unless you are shopping in a wine store that has expertise, how can you obtain information about the various wines available to you? Can you trust the little "shelf talkers" taped to the racks? Probably not, since they are often composed by the wholesaler or the wineries themselves. These are hardly objective sources of information. A shelf talker in a store with expertise might point you to a wine worth buying, if someone from the store has written it. (In this case, you might see the store logo on the card.) It is quite likely that the store bought a lot of a good wine, and they want to move the wine and make you a satisfied customer.

Assuming that you can't get any good information from a store worker or display, however, here are some useful tips to help you make a choice:

- **Know a grape:** If you like Sauvignon Blanc but can't find your favorite bottle, you might want to try a bottle from a different producer.
- **Know a region:** If the Cabernet you like is from Alexander Valley, California, try a different Cabernet from that same region. Remember, climate and soil (*terroir*) play a big part in winemaking.
- **Know a producer:** If you like Pride Mountain Merlot, you

might like Pride Mountain Cabernet Sauvignon, because the wine producer probably makes both types with the same winemaking philosophy.

- **Go to a wine tasting:** If you have enough interest in wine that you've made it this far into the book, then you owe it to yourself to attend a free wine tasting, which are often held at wine stores. Certainly, tasting a wine without having first to buy it is a worthwhile opportunity.

Wine for Entertaining a Crowd

Let's say 50 (or 250) of your friends or relatives are getting together for an informal dinner or even a cocktail party with hors d'oeuvres and wine. Because of your interest in wine, you've been put in charge of getting the wine for the event . . . it sounds daunting, but it is really quite simple.

They Call Them "Crowd-Pleasers" for a Reason

A large gathering of guests who probably don't know each other very well is not a good place to show off your wine expertise. Save the obscure Alsace Gewürztraminer and the puckery Portuguese red for your next wine tasting with friends, and stick to wines with broad appeal—crowd pleasers—for big events. Chardonnay and Merlot from California (or even Washington State) conform to most people's idea of a decent glass of wine, but you needn't confine yourself to just these two wines. For instance, an Italian-themed gathering would probably appreciate good varietal Sangiovese and Pinot Grigio. No matter what type of party you're having, you would always do well to have some White Zinfandel on hand in addition to your dry red and white choices. Make sure to choose a red and a white that are similarly priced so that one group or the other doesn't feel slighted. Buying a red and a white from the same producer that are the same price ("line-priced" in retail-speak) lends some uniformity to an event.

Establish a Budget and Calculate Your Needs

Choosing the wines is a simple matter once you know how much you are authorized to spend. Try to deal with a store that will not only give you a significant quantity discount but will also take back for credit any unopened bottles! This will take the guesswork out of your purchase. Just make sure that overenthusiastic servers or helpers don't open more bottles than necessary. You can't do much with a box of half-empty bottles the next day. Figure on at least half a (750ml) bottle per person, divided evenly between red and white. Remember, as long as the store will take back the extras, you can aim high.

Wine for a Wedding

Many couples are forgoing elaborate and expensive wedding receptions in favor of catering their own. Unless you are either very rich, or consider a banquet hall to be a worthy charity, you might consider doing this, especially after you find out how much you can save on the champagne and wine. As far as the wine is concerned, the only difference between a wedding and other large gatherings is the greater likelihood that champagne or other sparkling wine will be offered.

If the bubbly will only be used for a toast and perhaps a refill for some people, the calculations for the quantity needed are relatively straightforward—one bottle for every six people will give everyone a four-ounce pour. In order to pour accurate amounts and serve everyone faster, it is better to fill the glasses at a service bar and then deliver them from trays, rather than fill the glasses at the table.

You Need Glasses!

If you're throwing a big party, spend a little money and rent some decent wine glasses, because fancy wine in a plastic cup doesn't usually taste as good as slightly less expensive wine in a real wine glass. Wine glasses and champagne "flutes" cost about 30 cents each to rent; therefore, assuming each glass is refilled once, you could pay for the glassware rental by downgrading the cost of the wine you're serving by only 75 cents per bottle.

Ice Is Nice

Nobody has ever had *too* much ice for a party. Most household refrigerators aren't powerful enough to chill a lot of wine on short notice, and ice—lots of it—is the best way to chill large quantities of beverages for a party. You can spend too much money on those little two-gallon bags of ice. It would be great if you are friendly enough with your favorite restaurant that you could arrange in advance to pick up a picnic cooler or two full of ice from them the morning of your party. Alternatively, a brand-new garbage can with a plastic bag liner works well enough (as long as nobody throws garbage in it!).

Wine for Small Dinner Parties

A small dinner party of eight-to-twelve people is a perfect way to show off your cooking skills—and your ability to match interesting wines with each course.

Keep It Simple

Your house is not a restaurant with the space and equipment to put out hundreds of plates of food in one night, so try to keep the menu to a manageable size. Likewise, your guests are coming to enjoy each other's company as well as the food and wine—and then drive home safely. Keeping the number of different wines to no more than three is a good idea.

Plan Your Lineup

A lineup of three dinner party wines might go like this:

- Sparkling wine (with hors d'oeuvres)
- White wine (with a light first course)
- Red (with the main course)

If you are not having a "light first course" but instead are jumping right to the main course, eliminating one wine affords you the opportunity to offer an interesting dessert wine later on, something even many wine lovers rarely get to try. Of course, a perfectly good dinner party can certainly be built around fewer than three wines.

No matter how many wines you serve, remember that you will need the right glassware for each wine. Here's a quick run-down of glassware, courtesy of Cork Cuisine (*www.corkcuisine.com*).

- **White wine glasses** have a shape that looks a lot like a tulip. These all-purpose glasses can also be used to serve sparkling or red wine. Just remember that you should never serve white wine in a red wine glass.

- **Red wine glasses** are usually larger than their white coun-terparts. They have a rounder bowl, which enhances the wine's aroma because it allows for more air contact.
- **Flutes** are used to serve sparkling wines or champagne. These tall, thin glasses work best to bring out the delicate scent and effervescence of the wine. (Dessert-wine glasses are similar in shape to flutes.)
- **Dessert glasses** are like smaller white wine glasses.

Remember that any style of wine glass should always be held by the stem. Aesthetically speaking, this keeps fingerprints off of the glass, but, more importantly, it also prevents the wine from heating up too much. If you're in need of a good all-purpose wine glass, look for one that holds at least 10 ounces and curves in at the top. This helps the wine to hold its scent.

Make It Interesting

"Crowd pleasers" are appropriate for a large gathering, but a small dinner party calls for less recognized wines with some pizzazz. For example, serving a highly rated new release of a special wine would give your guests a fun way to gauge their tastes against that of a professional reviewer, and wine from an unusual grape variety or a lesser-known producer will make the whole experience more inter-esting and memorable.

Be Flexible

In spite of all the thought you might put into matching the right wines with each course, one or more of your guests might prefer to drink only the white (or only the red) throughout the meal. No problem—just make sure you have enough of each wine to allow for this option.

"House Wine" for Everyday Sipping

If you are one of the growing number of Americans who enjoy a glass or two of wine every night with dinner, you might want to consider choosing a "house wine" to purchase in quantity and keep on hand. This way, you'll save both money and time.

Narrow Your Search

A good reason for buying a mixed case (besides saving 15 percent) is that it gives you a chance to try different wines in your style and price range before you commit to a particular bottling. A knowledgeable wine merchant should gladly help you assemble some choices. You might spend more on "house wine," you might spend less, but there are a great number of choices, both red and white, available for around $10 . . . *before* your case discount!

If you like light, crisp whites, the best bargains in that category usually come from Italy. Excellent versions of Verdicchio, Orvieto, and even Pinot Grigio are available for $10 or less. If you like drier versions of Chardonnay, the *vin de pays d'oc* wines of Southern France are often good values. Some of the best examples of fruity Chardonnay you'll find for your money come from large producers in California and Australia. Look also to Australia for fruity reds such as Shiraz, which is very hard to beat for the price. As mentioned, the South of France (the Languedoc region) has a few good inexpensive whites, but it is a gold mine for good, inexpensive reds, as is Southern Italy.

The Apulia and Abruzzi regions in Italy's southeastern corner offer a variety of dry, earthy reds for less than the price of a pizza.

Save the Rest

If you want to serve only half of a bottle each evening, buy yourself a half-bottle of a wine you like, then wash out the empty bottle with spring water and save the cork. Now, next time you open a full bottle, pour half of it into the clean half-bottle (where, tightly corked, it will keep for at least a week) and enjoy the rest of the full bottle you opened.

Stocking a Wine Cellar

Imagine being able to head to your own wine cellar for the perfect bottle of wine. For a dedicated wine lover, a well-stocked cellar has several advantages over running out to the store every time:

- The wines are purchased by the case, at a discount.
- You can always have your favorites.
- You can enjoy older vintages.
- And you can brag about having a wine cellar!

A "wine cellar" doesn't have to be a brick-lined, candlelit room full of ancient, priceless bottles. It doesn't even have to be in the cellar! A closet will do, so long as the storage area meets the following conditions:

- It's dark (constant light may be harmful over time).
- It's cool (between 50° and 65°F throughout the year).

- It's dry (excessive humidity might encourage mold).
- But it's not too dry (a little humidity prevents the corks from drying out).
- Finally, you must be able to store the wines on their sides, once again, to keep the corks moist.

Of course, you still have to come up with the wines you actually want to keep. Here are some useful guidelines for choosing wines to put in your cellar.

Wines to Keep on Hand for Company

Wouldn't it be great to be able to pull out a nice bottle of wine whenever you need it, to offer company that stops by on short notice? Reds and whites in the $15 to $20 range, a little more special than your everyday wines, are great to have on hand. To fill this niche, you should look for the following wines in the above price range:

- A Californian Chardonnay
- A Merlot or other fruity red
- A Pinot Grigio
- A Chianti

Wines to Keep on Hand for Special Occasions

Every now and then, a special day sneaks up on you. Whether it's an anniversary or an impromptu dinner party, here are some special wines that will fit the bill nicely:

- Californian Cabernet Sauvignon that you've aged for a couple of years.
- Carefully chosen red Burgundy or Oregon Pinot Noir.

- Less expensive *cru classé* Bordeaux or one of the better of the *cru bourgeois* Bordeaux.
- Maybe a fancy first- or second-growth Bordeaux for a *very* special occasion.
- Your favorite Champagne (the real thing, from France).
- A good dessert wine.

Wines Worth Aging

Not all wines benefit from a few years of aging; in fact, more and more premium producers are making "modern-style" wines that are fruitier and more enjoyable in their youth than the wines that they produced in the past. That being said, there are a great number of wines that benefit from aging in your wine cellar for a few years:

- Cabernet Sauvignon
- Châteauneuf-du-Pape
- Northern Rhônes, such as Hermitage
- Red Bordeaux
- German Rieslings
- Port and other dessert wines
- Barolo and Barbaresco from Piedmont
- Super-Tuscans, Brunello di Montalcino, Vino Nobile di Montepulciano, and riserva Chiantis from Tuscany

This list is by no means complete. Most wine reviewers give the aging potential of wines in their reviews, and a surprising number of wines—even whites—are deemed worthy of at least some short-term cellaring.

Wine to Put Away for a Child's Twenty-First Birthday

Your newborn first child just came home, and you want to put some wine from his birth year away for his twenty-first birthday. Relax . . . the truly ageworthy reds won't be released for a few years. However, your choices for wines that will reliably keep for two decades are narrow. Vintage port and classified-growth Bordeaux are probably the two safest choices. Port producers don't "declare" a vintage until two years have passed, so you have time to wait and see. If the vintage reports from Bordeaux are enthusiastic in the year of your child's birth, you'll also have to wait a couple of years to buy the wine . . . unless you buy it on futures.

Buying Wine Futures

You know you've crossed the line from a casual wine buff to a serious wine collector when you start buying wine futures. This involves committing to the purchase of a particular wine by paying for it up front and then receiving the wine maybe two years later. The best reason for doing this is that you will get the wine of your choice at a price far less than you ever would if you waited for the wine to be released. You can buy wine futures through any retailer who offers them, but make sure that it is a long-established business—one that you are willing to trust with your money for two years. There have been cases of shady retailers taking money for wine futures and then vanishing.

The wine part of the deal is not as risky as it might sound. In years when Bordeaux is blessed with a warm, dry growing season and a rain-free harvest, the top producers in Bordeaux can be counted on to produce excellent and ageworthy wine.

Chapter 12

Navigating the Restaurant Wine List

IF CHOOSING THE RIGHT WINE for dinner at home is stressful, ordering the right wine from a restaurant's wine list can be downright intimidating. The wine selections available in restaurants often include older vintages, limited-production wines, and other hard-to-find treasures. Wine is also considerably more expensive in restaurants than in wine stores.

Buying Wine in a Restaurant

Once you become familiar with various types of wine and figure out what kinds you really like, there is not that much more to know about buying wine in a restaurant . . . except that it costs a lot more. The more you learn about wine, the more painfully aware you become of the prices of wine in restaurants. If you enjoy going to restaurants and want to enjoy wine when you are there, consider the following:

1. Food is often marked up more than wine.

Good restaurants usually mark up food about three and a half times. In other words, a $20 entree probably costs the restaurant about $6 to prepare. While some restaurants mark up their wine just as much as their food, most restaurants charge around double their wholesale cost for mid-priced wines. A restaurant adds expertise and convenience when preparing the raw ingredients of your entree. Insist on the same with your wine—proper serving temperature (see Chapter 6, Wine Flaws), sparkling clean and appropriate glassware, and attentive service are all essential to a pleasurable wine-drinking experience in restaurants.

2. If nobody bought wine, there would be fewer restaurants.

Most restaurants need wine sales to survive. If you enjoy dining at a particular restaurant, your wine purchases will help to keep it there.

3. You can send it back . . . within reason.

If a wine has gone bad or suffers from cork spoilage, any restaurant should gladly take it back. If a wine steward or waiter has enthusiastically recommended a wine and you don't like it, you should also be allowed to return it.

But if you simply don't like a wine, step back a bit. Do others at your table agree? Have you tasted it without food? If so, taste it with a well-chewed piece of bread in your mouth. Wine is meant to be tasted with food. Might it need to breathe? If you aren't sure, ask the waiter to pour some wine into a glass, and let it breathe for a few minutes. If you still just don't like it, a good restaurant will probably try to keep you happy, especially if you are a regular customer. It is best not to make a habit of this practice, however.

By the way, most wines sent back in restaurants go back to the supplier, thus relieving the restaurant of the cost. The exception to this is older wine.

Older Wine

Let's say you're in a restaurant and you order a twenty-year-old Bordeaux. This wine might have been in the restaurant's cellar for fifteen years. At $100 a bottle, you have a right to expect good, solid wine. However, can you send it back if, while showing no flaws, it fails to live up to your expectations? Probably, but you should consider that the price of older wine often reflects its scarcity rather than its intrinsic value. You pay a premium for the opportunity to enjoy wine on your twentieth anniversary from, say, the year of your marriage. So be thoughtful about returning such wines. In this case, the restaurant will probably have to eat the cost of the bottle. (Depending on when they bought it, this might be a surprisingly small amount of money.)

Wine by the Glass Is Often Very Expensive

In restaurants, the markup on bottles of wine is far less than the markup on mixed drinks. Because many customers now order a glass of wine in place of that initial cocktail, smart restaurant operators ensure that they make the same money on that drink and mark up wine by the glass accordingly. Premium wine by the glass is a better value, a category in which the markup is more in line with the wine program than with the martini program. These premium wines by the glass are a convenient service for those who can't agree on a bottle or don't want to drink that much.

Know the Price Structure

In a retail store, you can calculate the price of wines very easily. In most cases, the wine costs about 50 percent over wholesale. After a few shopping trips, you will know what the most commonly sold wines in your area cost on the wholesale level.

The Magic Rule

In a good restaurant with fairly priced food and wine, wine that is as good as the food will cost about twice the price of the average entree. ~◇~

Good restaurants often mark up their best and most expensive wines at a lower rate than their inexpensive choices. This policy encourages customers to "trade up" for better value. Some restaurant owners, however, simply triple the wholesale cost of every wine, making them uniformly double the usual retail price.

Making a Selection

This is the fun part! Ordering a bottle with which you are familiar is the safest option; however, many of California's finest treasures are available only to fine restaurants. You might have read glowing reviews of such wines, only to find them impossible to purchase from a wine merchant. It follows that you won't get after-the-fact sticker shock by spotting such a gem on a retail shelf for far less than the restaurant's price.

Restaurant lists are also likely to offer older vintages of special reds worthy of cellaring. It makes no financial sense for a retail store to age wine, but wines from older vintages—perhaps a "vertical" (multiple vintages) of a particular producer—can draw wine buffs to a restaurant. And so you might order a special bottle that is unavailable anywhere else, or a mature red from an old vintage . . . or just an inexpensive bottle to accompany your meal.

Know Your Comfort Level

Everyone who buys wine develops a price point in their mind beyond which they are not comfortable, for fear that they will not appreciate a wine's value. The more you learn about wine, the more this price point will go up. ❧

A table of four might have ordered fish, pasta, chicken, and steak, and finding the "perfect wine" might be impossible. You don't need to. Most restaurants with well-managed wine programs offer half-bottles, and a table of four can easily enjoy two different wines at the same time.

Finally, a restaurant wine program is only as good as its service, and a professional wine steward should be on the staff in a well-run establishment. It is his or her job to know something about every wine on the list, and to be able to describe it to you accurately. The days of the snooty, intimidating, and condescending wine steward

Enjoying Wine with Your Dinner

Just as at home, in a restaurant you have some control over the enjoyment of your wine. Is this white too cold? Let it warm up on the table and in the glass, and taste the hidden flavors as they emerge. Is the red too warm? Your server should cool it for you in ice water for five minutes or so. Your server should also be pouring the wine for you—in proper glassware, never more than half full—though it is okay to pour it yourself. Don't drink it all before the food arrives (unless you're planning to buy another bottle, of course).

are thankfully over, now that wine has become a more integral part of our culture. Accordingly, you should be able to rely on the wine steward's advice if you have any questions. Offering the wine steward a small taste of your wine is an excellent way to show your gratitude while contributing to his or her continuing education.

The Wine Ritual

In restaurants, there is a certain ritual of procedure that takes place when wine is served. You order the wine, and you are shown the label. Is it the right year? If you ordered a "reserve," make sure it is not a lesser bottling from the same producer. So far, so good. Tell the server to keep the cork, unless you collect corks; it is of no use to you once you have verified that it hasn't rotted during its years in the bottle. Do taste the wine while the server is there. Any problem should be addressed immediately. Your server should then pour wine for everyone at the table.

How Should You Tip?

Many people treat tipping on wine as a separate issue. There's no need to do so. You might argue that the same effort applies to serving a $100 bottle as a $20 bottle, and, therefore, you need not tip a full 15 percent on the more expensive wine. (However, the same reasoning, if applied to tipping on an expensive entree versus tipping on a cup of soup, would be foolish.) Save the math problems for another time and just tip on the whole bill, with maybe an extra $5 to $10 to the wine steward (or server) for an especially enjoyable recommendation.

An alternative tipping strategy is to tip 20 percent on your food and 10 to 15 percent on your restaurant wine purchases.

Can You Bring Your Own Bottle (BYOB)?

This is an ongoing debate between some (but not all) restaurant owners and serious wine collectors. The restaurateurs argue that selling wine for a profit is an essential part of their business, just as selling food is. If they allow customers to bring in their own wine, they reason, they lose out on profits. Why not just let customers bring their own food as well? The pro-BYOB faction, meanwhile, argues that restaurant wine prices are outrageously high, and that many wine connoisseurs would fill the restaurants' empty seats if they were permitted to bring their cellar treasures to enjoy with a well-prepared restaurant meal.

A compromise position is the "corkage fee," a price added to the dinner bill of those customers who bring their own wine. This fee helps to offset the lost profit on a wine sale and the costs of maintaining glassware. Corkage fees of $10 or even $20 are reasonable. Ironically, there are stories of some fancy restaurants charging $100 or more, which is as predatory as many of the wine list prices that inspire customers to bring their own bottles in the first place.

Here are some points of BYOB etiquette:

- Always ask ahead of time if BYOB is allowed. (It is actually illegal in some states.) Know the corkage fee beforehand as well.
- It is rude to bring a bottle that is already on the restaurant's wine list. If you're going to BYOB, bring something special.
- Remember that it costs the waiter a wine tip when you bring your own.
- Offer the wine steward a taste of your special wine—this just might get your corkage fee waived.

- Remember that restaurants are not government-subsidized picnic areas for your wine enjoyment. They are in business to make money, and they are doing you a favor when they let you BYOB.

The Bottom Line

Unless you care to cook elaborate meals for yourself and your guests on a regular basis, paying restaurant prices for wine is unavoidable. When ordering wine in a restaurant, we recommend taking the opportunity to enjoy special wines that are otherwise unavailable to you. Knowledge is power—having some idea of what "restaurant only" wines actually cost the restaurant is obviously useful and can often be inferred from published ratings.

Chapter 13

Wine and Food

FOOD AND WINE HAVE ALWAYS BEEN a great combination at the dinner table. Meals that include wine have come to symbolize good times. Here is a partial list of reasons, past and present, why people enjoy wine and food together:

1. Few beverage options existed when wine became part of food culture centuries ago.
2. Pure drinking water has not always been widely available.
3. With its high acidity and other properties, wine assists in the digestion of food.
4. Certain wines are so delicious with certain foods that they seem made for each other.
5. When a meal is served as a celebration or holiday feast, the alcohol in wine raises everyone's spirits.
6. If a couple is sharing a romantic meal, wine seems to enhance the intimacy.

7. Water is boring.
8. If you don't drink anything when you eat, the food might get stuck.

You can think of other good reasons for matching wine with food. Of course, just as you can enjoy food without wine, you can enjoy many wines without food. Sweet wines, wines naturally low in alcohol, and low-acid wines are easy to enjoy by themselves. Rich, chewy wines might be too flavorful for your taste at the dinner table. You'll want to drink them at other times. And, of course, drinking a favorite wine alone is always pleasurable without food.

Matching Food and Wine

Since food and wine are so enjoyable together, it should be a fairly simple matter to match them. Unfortunately, it is doubtful that any dining ritual has caused more anxiety than that of choosing the "correct pairing." What a shame! We're talking about two very enjoyable things, after all: good food and good wine. Unless you make a fundamental error and choose a pairing that results in an unpleasant chemical reaction in your mouth—an error that is 100-percent avoidable, by the way—you can't go wrong. With a little effort and forethought, you can pair wine and food so that they make each other taste even better!

The Golden Rule

Many people are familiar with the old, well-established rule of food/wine pairing: "White wine with fish, red wine with meat." While this rule is not as valid as it once was (this chapter will show you why), the reasoning behind it is sound, and it deserves examination.

Think of a nice, fresh fillet of fish, neatly grilled or broiled. Most of us who enjoy fish would welcome a squeeze of fresh lemon on it. Why? The acid in the lemon "cuts" the intrinsic fish flavor without overpowering it. Thus, white wine, with its more apparent acidity and less powerful flavors, would be more appropriate for sole than red wine.

Now imagine a roast of beef with delicious gravy made from onions and pan drippings. The assertive flavor of the gravy matches in magnitude the flavor of the beef, as would a rich red wine. Just as onion gravy would overwhelm the fillet of sole, so would most red wines. And just as a squeeze of lemon would be lost on the roast beef, so too would most white wines. If only it were that simple.

Culinary Considerations from France

Chef August Escoffier (1846–1935) is widely regarded as the father of French cuisine. French cuisine, in turn, is the mother lode of fine cookery in Western civilization. Thus, for many decades it was a truism that the finest restaurant in any American city was a French-inspired restaurant with a menu that Escoffier could have written himself. In his authoritative culinary writings, Escoffier thoughtfully dictated the accompaniments and sauces for each entree of the repertoire classique. Matching a wine to the meal was relatively straightforward; the French wine list covered all the bases.

Although Escoffier's teachings are still relevant today, he lived, cooked, and wrote in a time before reliable refrigeration and easy transportation. The world of fine cookery has evolved accordingly. Where French restaurants once reigned supreme, we now find Thai,

Brazilian, Northern Italian, and Moroccan restaurants of equal stature. But perhaps Escoffier's most enduring gift is the ability of French cuisine to adopt and incorporate such varying influences. If he were alive today, he might stumble upon a "fusion" restaurant that blends many international influences, often on the same plate. If it were thoughtfully and competently prepared, Escoffier would undoubtedly approve . . . But he might have trouble choosing a wine.

Tips for Pairing Wine with Food

Among the changes in fine cookery since Escoffier's time, the increasing complexity of food is the most troublesome when it comes to matching it with wine. Here are some guidelines (*not rules*).

1. Don't dwell on color. There are enough other factors to consider; the color will take care of itself. For instance, chicken dishes can be prepared to match well with any wine, depending on the ingredients. Lighter reds and strong whites can survive most food pairings.

2. Match strengths. Powerfully flavored dishes require wines of equal fortitude. For example, herb-crusted leg of lamb or garlicky ratatouille match well with a strongly flavored wine, usually red. On the other hand, delicate dishes need delicate wine. Simply prepared white fish like sole, for instance, needs a gentle wine, usually white.

3. Opposites attract. For example, the spicy cuisine of the Pacific Rim needs a light, sweet wine to extinguish the fire. Rich cream or butter sauces are well matched with an acidic, "cutting wine."

4. Regional affinity. In Europe it is a truism that regional cooking goes best with the local wine. Since gastronomy and oenology evolved side by side, it stands to reason that food and wine derived from the same soil and served on the same dinner table have an underlying affinity.

5. Pair simple wine with complex food. This would solve the hypothetical dilemma of Escoffier in a "fusion" restaurant. Pair this food with a varietal not inclined to great complexity—Pinot Blanc (among whites) and Merlot (among reds) come to mind.

6. Serve complex wine with simple food. The best way to showcase a fabulously complex (and expensive) wine is to pair it with a simple, yet delicious, background dish. Examples include a super-premium Cabernet Sauvignon with plain grilled steak or a great white Burgundy (Chardonnay) with plain broiled fish.

7. Match price. A $70 Brunello di Montalcino would be wasted on a pizza, but a carefully prepared dinner deserves an equally special wine, not a pizza wine.

8. Sparkling wine still goes with almost anything . . . Because the bubbles make up for the lightness of flavor, sparkling wine can be perfectly fine with traditional red-wine dishes.

9. . . . And so does rosé. Wine snobs are quick to dismiss rosé. If it tastes good, drink it. Although it is not really "right" with any food, it isn't really "wrong" either, unless you don't like rosé.

10. Match wine to the occasion. Rosé is frequently referred to as a "picnic wine." Informal gatherings call for informal wine. Save the haughty bottles for three-fork dinner parties.

11. You can serve red wine with fish. As long as the acid level is high and the tannins are barely noticeable, red wine is fine with most seafood. Here are some suggestions:

- Simple Chianti or other Sangiovese-based Italian wine.
- Certain Pinot Noirs: Côte de Beaune, Chalonnais, Oregon, lighter California Beaujolais, or other Gamay-based wines.

- Lighter versions of Merlot (or Merlot blends), particularly Saint-Emilion (Bordeaux).
- Spanish Rioja: Though often not so high in acid, the lighter of these Tempranillo-based wines are usually versatile enough for seafood.

12. You can also serve white wine with beef. Certain whites are big enough to stand up to charred sirloin and other beef dishes. Consider high-alcohol and well-oaked California or Australian Chardonnay. Viognier-based whites are up for the challenge as well. This offbeat varietal can be one of the most pleasant surprises in the wine world.

13. Serve cheaper wines with cheese. The fat in cheese makes wine taste better. This makes cheese an important ingredient for receptions at which large quantities of inexpensive wine are served.

14. Fruit and wine don't match. Most fruits are acidic, and so are most wines. Fruit acids can throw a good wine out of balance. Fruit is acceptable as a garnish for cheap "champagne," but not real Champagne from France or anything like it. The one possible exception to this rule is sparkling wine, with its prominent acidity, which often lends itself to a festive and decorative touch of fresh fruit, such as strawberries.

However, it is almost impossible to pair dry wine and fruit successfully. Assuming that the wine is well-made (and thus in balance) the fruit will only throw it out of balance. Aside from berries in bubbly, about the only other exception to this truism is fruit that can attain extreme ripeness, such as a perfect pear, or fruit as an accompaniment to a rich and sweet dessert wine.

15. Wine and chocolate don't match. And they never will, although it's fun to try!

You Don't Always Need to Match

So you love salmon and you love Cabernet Sauvignon . . . Fine! Have them together. A sip of water and a nibble of bread will smooth the transition from one to the other. There are a few caveats, however. Beware of serving wine with known wine-killers—namely, artichokes, eggs, avocados, peanuts, asparagus, and chili peppers. These are among the most troublesome food ingredients, as they react negatively with any wine in your mouth. Crisp, dry Sauvignon Blanc is a good wine to have with green vegetables that might react unfavorably with other wines and, thus, is as good a wine as any to serve with a known wine-killer. Sweet Riesling can coexist with hot and spicy flavors that obliterate most wines, but it is certainly a shotgun wedding at best with painfully spicy food that would be more enjoyable with cold beer.

White Wine with Red Meat (Anti-Match #1)

Let's say you're in a fancy steakhouse with another couple, and you all want steak and white wine . . . is this a sommelier's nightmare? Not really. There are some strapping Chardonnays from California's Sonoma and Napa regions that can climb in the ring with just about any meat dish and still hold their own. The secret is wood, an important component of any big California Chardonnay. Ripe Chardonnay fruit, high alcohol, and a glycerine-charged body benefit from aging in new oak, which seems to unify these powerful components while adding a touch of tannin and further complexity. Australian and Santa Barbara Chardonnays also qualify, but they are likely to show more fruit than wood. Big French Chardonnays from the Côte de Beaune are another possibility, but their higher acidity and more subtle charms might be lost on red meat.

If you are less interested in the wine than the food, any subtle white wine can be served. However, the wine's flavors won't be easily noticed.

Red Wine with Fish (Anti-Match #2)

This is a hip way to break the rules, especially with something like a tuna or swordfish steak. Look for high-acid, low-tannin wines—Italian reds tend to be versatile, as are Pinot Noirs from Oregon and Burgundy. California Pinot Noir might be a little too fruity. Rioja might be okay with fish. French Saint-Emilion, in which Merlot usually predominates, is a light take on a fruity grape and a decent match with fish.

In general, European wines are crafted to be food friendly. This is good to remember when you are trying to make an unorthodox food/wine match such as fish with red wine.

If you go with a red that is powerfully flavored, you'll end up missing most of the fish's flavor. If you have a wine that is too strong for your fish, or any meal, put it aside and drink it after you eat. The better the fish, the more you'll want to preserve the food experience.

As a general rule, fish that is grilled takes on a charred flavor that makes it more compatible with red wines than white. It stands to reason that the fish we usually grill are quite flavorful to begin with—salmon, tuna, swordfish, and shark.

Good Wine and Food Matches

If you're stumped about the right wine to serve with the food you prepare at your next dinner party, or you draw a blank every time you need to decide on an appropriate wine to drink with your meal at a restaurant, read on.

Red Meat Dishes

Food	Wine
Chili con carne	Beaujolais (an easy-drinking red); Zinfandel (a red to stand up to your chili)
Grilled steak	Cabernet Sauvignon (an ultimate match); Shiraz/Syrah (a good choice at a better price)
Hamburger	Any red wine you like that is inexpensive
Roast beef	Pinot Noir and Merlot (softer reds than for your grilled steak). If you are wild about Cabernet Sauvignon, then have a Cabernet from Bordeaux
Steak au poivre (steak with black peppercorn sauce)	BIG REDS: Zinfandel from California and Rhône reds are perfect
Tenderloin	Same as for roast beef: Pinot Noir and Merlot are the good choices

Poultry Dishes

Food	Wine
Chicken (roasted)	Almost any wine you like—this is a very versatile dish
Chicken (highly seasoned)	Chenin Blanc, Riesling, or other unoaked white
Turkey	Rosé, sweet or dry; rich and heavy whites
Duck and goose	Pinot Blanc or Viognier among whites and Merlot or Rhônes among reds
Game Birds	Pinot Noir

Other Meat Dishes

Food	Wine
Ham	Rosé; fruity Pinot Noir; Pinot Gris; Gewürztraminer
Lamb (simple)	Cabernet (especially from Bordeaux); Rioja red from Spain
Lamb (with herbs and garlic)	Cabernet Sauvignon, Spanish reds, Rhônes
Pork	A light Italian or Spanish red; Viognier, Pinot Gris, Gewürztraminer or some other rich white
Sausage	Gewürztraminer or a rustic red
Veal	Richer whites, such as Chardonnay; light reds
Venison (deer)	A big red wine: Cabernet, Nebbiolo, Syrah, or Zinfandel will do well

Seafood Dishes

Food	Wine
Anything with a cream sauce	White Burgundy (clean, crisp Chardonnay)
Lobster	Champagne; dry Riesling; white Burgundy
Oysters	Muscadet, a French white, is ideal with oysters; Chablis (dry French Chardonnay) or Champagne
Salmon	Sauvignon Blanc
Shrimp	Light and dry white wine
Swordfish	Light to medium white wines of all sorts
Tuna	This fish is versatile like chicken; anything but a big red is okay; a light red is probably the ideal match
White fish (sole, for instance)	Sauvignon Blanc, light Chardonnay

Pasta Dishes

Food	Wine
Red sauce	Barbera; Chianti or another Sangiovese-based red
Vegetables	Grüner Veltliner, Sauvignon Blanc, or other crisp whites
White sauce	Pinot Grigio

Some General Food-Wine Categories

Category	Characteristics	Examples
Fish Whites	Crisp, light and acidic	Muscadet, Macon, Pinot Grigio, Sauvignon Blanc
Turkey Whites	Rich and heavy whites to accompany holiday meals	Viognier, Pinot Gris, Gewürztraminer
Fish Reds	Light and acidic reds with little tannin	Sangiovese, Lighter Barbera, Lighter Spanish reds, Lighter Merlot, Red Burgundy, and other Pinot Noir
Peppersteak Reds	Big, bold reds that stand up to strongly flavored dishes	Châteauneuf-du-Pape, Cabernet Sauvignon, Malbec, Syrah/Shiraz

Enjoying Wine Without Food

If you like wine and you're not hungry, you can either wait until you have an appetite again, or just enjoy a glass of wine on its own. If you buy wine to be enjoyed without food, keep the following in mind.

1. Low-acid wine is better. High-acid wines need food to show well. The unmitigated acidity of many classic food wines is such that they cannot be enjoyed alone. Remember, acidity helps quench a thirst and cuts through the starch and fleshiness of food. A fruity Pinot Noir or Chardonnay from California will certainly go well solo, as will an Australian Chardonnay or Shiraz/Cabernet blend.

2. Have your white wine a bit warmer than usual. Good white wine is best at 45°–50°F (8°–10°C), which is warmer than your refrigerator. Without food to focus on, you can ponder the complexities of a good white wine, which reveal themselves more at warmer temperatures. If you open a bottle and let it warm over time, you can observe the wine at different temperatures. Try a white you know you like, and learn its secrets.

3. Have your red wine a little cooler than usual. A slight chill takes the edge off the acidity and makes the wine more soothing on the tongue.

4. Avoid big, tannic wines. Unless tannin turns you on, a lot of tannin will be more overbearing without food. Save that special Cabernet for the dinner table, or at least the cheese-and-cracker table.

5. Sweetness is okay. If you have always avoided anything but dry wines, you might want to try an off-dry wine for a change. German Riesling, Vouvray demi-sec, and California Gewürztraminers, Rieslings, and rosés are all wines that don't require food in order to show their best qualities.

6. Now is the time to try a fortified wine. Dry or sweet, light or dark, you can't go wrong. Remember that the fortified wines—Port, Sherry, Madeira, and Marsala—are fortified with alcohol, so you will be sipping, not gulping.

7. Sweeter and sparkling. Off-dry Champagnes and sparkling wines that don't go well at the dinner table are quite enjoyable without food. Fruity, off-dry, sparkling wines are quite enjoyable without food.

Cooking with Wine

Many French or French-inspired recipes call for wine as an ingredient. Food and wine have a wonderful affinity at the table, and in the kitchen as well. The wine you cook with needs to be drinkable, but certainly not great. Here's a common-sense rule: If you wouldn't drink it, don't cook with it. This rules out the overpriced, denatured "cooking wine" found in supermarkets next to the Worcestershire sauce.

Restaurants sometimes use the name of a wine on the menu in order to market a dish. You may see "Pinot Noir Sauce" or "Champagne Beurre Blanc" in the menu description. This is unreliable. If the wines used in these recipes were that great, the restaurant would be serving them by the glass, not by the ladle. Some swank restaurants might actually say "Dom Pérignon Sauce" on their specials menu, but chances are that such a wine was opened in error the night before. Always consider the "cachet value" factor when encountering anything wine-related at a restaurant.

Good chefs know how to choose good quality, cost-effective wines for cooking. Here is a list of frequently called-for cooking wines, and some tips for choosing them.

Dry White Wine

Look for simple, fruity yet dry table wines—Chardonnay or Sauvignon Blanc among the "fighting varietals" or other drinkable yet inexpensive wines. Avoid sharp, acidic wines, excessively woody wines, and sweet wines—all of these qualities become more concentrated during cooking.

Dry Red Wine

Lighter reds low in tannin work best.

Sherry

True Spanish Sherry adds considerable character when called for in a recipe. Avoid very dry fino Sherry and sweet cream Sherry. The safest choice is Amontillado, the light-amber-colored, medium-bodied Sherry.

Port

Ruby port, the least expensive type of Port, is probably the best for cooking. It is fruity and sweet, and will retain its color. Port is powerful stuff and should be used modestly in food. In addition to Ruby Ports from Portugal, Australian "Ports" tend to have a nutty sweetness reminiscent of Sherry that works well in cooking.

Madeira

There are no substitutes when a recipe calls for Madeira. Madeira is a key component of France's *Sauce Perigourdine*: a sinfully rich concoction of foie gras, truffles, and demi-glace. Madeira sauces have a particular affinity for beef, game, and mushroom dishes. For cooking, a medium-bodied Bual Madeira works best.

Marsala

This Sicilian fortified wine is a staple in Southern Italian cooking. The label on a Marsala bottle will indicate whether it is dry or sweet. Both work well in many recipes, although the sweet version is advisable for dessert sauces.

Vermouth

Always use white vermouth when cooking, never the sweeter red. The intense complex flavor of vermouth enhances many light seafood dishes. Good-quality white vermouth is widely available from Italy, France, and California.

Brandy

It is worth splurging for a relatively inexpensive Cognac of the "V.S." grade when a recipe calls for brandy. Cognac offers reliable and intense flavors and because "nip"-sized bottles of brandy (as well as other spirits that a recipe might call for) are readily available, this ingredient won't cost you a fortune.

Sparkling Wine

When you cook any sparkling wine, you will eliminate its primary qualities: bubbles and alcohol. In most cases, Champagne as an ingredient is useful for its cachet value only. However, a simple beurre blanc sauce can benefit from the two remaining qualities of good Champagne: high acidity and yeast flavor.

Pale Californian, Champagne-method sparkling wines are a good choice for cooking. These tend to have a tad more fruit than their French counterparts, which makes them a bit more flavorful in the saucepan.

Part 5

Resources

Web Site Reference Guide

NOW THAT YOU'VE LEARNED all of the basics you need to understand wine grapes and regions, select the right wine for your tastes, and shop for, order, and serve wine with the best of them, don't stop here. There is a wealth of information available on the Internet to help you expand and deepen your understanding of this extensive subject.

Wine Dictionaries and Reference Tools

Inevitably, there will be times when you encounter a new wine term you're not sure of or a particular brand of wine you'd like to know more about. Try these Web sites to expand your wine horizons.

Epicurious (*www.epicurious.com*): Click on the Drink selection of the Web site's home page, and you'll find a link to Epicurious's Essential Wine Guide, which offers recent articles, wine reviews, and recommendations. The main page of The Essential Wine Guide links to additional resources, including Epicurious's Wine Lover's Companion. Here, you'll find all sorts of details on types of wines, wine producers, wineries, a dictionary of terms, and more.

For specifics on Italian wines, try **The Wine Tool** (*www.thewinetool.com*), which features information on major producers, online wine stores, and extensive selections of wines. The site will also connect you to a wealth of information on other wines besides Italian selections, once you begin investigating the links.

The Wine Lover's Page (*www.wineloverspage.com*): An online magazine that features articles written by a variety of columnists, the site has discussion groups, a Wine Travel and Restaurants Forum, departments that include food and wine matching, vintage charts, favorite Internet links and books, lists of wine recommendations, and more.

The Vine Times (*www.thevinetimes.com*): This resource covers wine and related subjects, including food, travel, and lifestyle. The Wine 101 Basics section offers a link to wine regions and also provides useful information on individual wineries in California.

Expert Opinions

If you're interested in researching what the experts have to say about a broad variety of wines, the following two sites offer the best information:

Wine Spectator online (*www.winespectator.com*): *Wine Spectator's* wine school offers online courses; the site also features a travel section, vintage charts, ratings, daily wine news, and more. There is a membership fee and members must log in to access certain information. (Note that *Wine Spectator* takes advertising and, as such, wine experts are cautious when weighing this resource's input.)

Wine expert **Robert Parker's Web site** (*erobertparker.com*): This site also requires registration, but you can sign up for a free trial to test it out. Here, you're able to search a database of more than 60,000 tasting notes from Robert Parker's books and his newsletter, *The Wine Advocate.* Other resources include an article archive, educational links, vintage charts, a glossary of terms, and a find-it online option that helps users locate favorite wines at online wine merchants using price listings from Winealert.com.

Wine Retail Links

Sites that help you search for wines you can buy on the Internet abound. Here are a few of the most useful options:

If it's great online shopping you're after, check out **Wine.com** (*www.wine.com*). You can browse selections by type, region, or winery, and there are also links to top sellers as well as fine wines. This site offers gift baskets and gourmet food, too.

Having a hard time tracking down your favorite wine? **Wine Searcher** (*www.wine-searcher.com*) offers detailed and direct searching methods. Just pop in the wine's name and vintage, and you're set. If you're not so sure about what you're looking for, this site also provides links to recommended wines, top wine searches, and suggestions for good wines to give as gifts.

Wine Enthusiast (*www.wineenthusiast.com*): This online catalog is the place to go for wine accessories. Here, you'll find corkscrews, serving items, stemware, decanters, wine racks, serving and preserving tools, and other useful items. The site also features a recommendations page, as well as a gift guide.

Useful Industry Information

In case you're in need of more in-depth analysis on the wine industry, here are a few options:

Touted as "The Voice for California Wine" on its Web site homepage, **The Wine Institute** (*www.wineinstitute.org*) is the public policy advocacy association of California wineries. Wine Institute taps into the resources of 715 wineries and affiliated businesses in an effort to support legislative and regulatory advocacy, international market development, media relations, scientific research, and education programs to benefit California's wine industry. This site provides interesting statistics, news, information on wine sales and wine-growing practices, and more.

WineLinx.com (*www.winelinx.com*): An excellent resource for links to all sorts of wine organizations, associations, directories and publications, this site includes state wine associations and links to wineries and wine trails.

Regional Wineries

For information on locating regional wineries, try these resources:

Yahoo (*http://dir.yahoo.com*) features descriptions and contact information for selected wineries in the U.S., Europe, Australia and New Zealand, and Chile. Click Directory, Business and Economy, Shopping and Services, Food and Drink, Drinks, Alcohol and Spirits, Wine, Wineries, and then Directories.

Google's Web Directory (*http://directory.google.com*) also provides wine guides and directories. Click Recreation, Food, Drink, Wine,

Guides, and then Directories, and you can specify locations further from there.

Wines Northwest (*www.winesnw.com*), is an online guide to the wines and wineries of the Pacific Northwest. It features maps and information about the wine regions within Oregon, Washington, Idaho, and British Columbia. The site includes lists of Northwest wineries, wine shops, tour guides, and driving services, all organized within each region, along with nearby lodging and dining suggestions and a calendar of upcoming events.

For extensive information on California wine regions, as well as wine regions in other parts of the country, go to **Wine Country.com** (*www.winecountry.com*). You'll find individual links to California's Gold County, Mendocino County, Monterey County, Napa Valley, San Luis Obispo, Santa Barbara, Santa Cruz, Sonoma County, Temecula, and Lake County. Other wine regions explored include Virginia, Oregon, New York State, Texas, and Washington State. There are also search options, listings of events, newsletters, discounts, and promotions, among other things.

Uncork New York's Wine Country Web site (*www.nywine.com*): Click on the home page's Wine Country selection, and you'll link into the site's information on each of New York State's wine regions: Lake Erie, the Finger Lakes, Central New York, Hudson Valley, New York City, and Long Island. The site also features a Map Center, Event Center, Wine Locator option, and Information Station.

The French Wine Explorer's Web site (*www.wine-tours-france.com*) provides information on wine tours, trips, and current wine-vacation schedules in France. Information on the separate regions of Bordeaux, Burgundy, Champagne, Loire Valley, and Provence is available.

The Tuscan Sensations Web site (*www.tuscansensations.com*) offers links to Italian wineries, wine organizations and resources, information on Italian wines, and more.

The WineWeb (*www.wineweb.com*) is a great resource for locating wineries all over the world, by country. This site provides information on more than 20,000 wineries, and of these, more than 9,000 of them have their own winery Web sites integrated into The WineWeb. It's a pretty good bet that you'll find almost any location you're looking for here!

Bibliography

Adams, Leon D. *The Wines of America, 2nd Edition Revised.* New York: McGraw-Hill, 1978.

Anderson, Burton. *The Wine Atlas of Italy.* New York: Simon & Schuster, Inc., 1990.

Asher, Gerald. *Vineyard Tales: Reflections on Wine.* San Francisco: Chronicle Books, 1996.

Johnson, Hugh. *The World Atlas of Wine: A Complete Guide to the Wines and Spirits of the World.* New York: Simon & Schuster, Inc., 1971.

Robinson, Jancis, ed. *The Oxford Edited Companion to Wine.* Oxford, New York: Oxford University Press, 1994.

Glossary

A

AC/AOC: An abbreviation for Appellation d'Origine Contrôlée, the set of French wine laws that has established winemaking standards for quality French wines. AC is the top level of quality; VDQS is a set of laws with slightly lower standards; *vin de pays* is a lower yet standard; and *vin de table* is the lowest set of standards.

ACETIC: Vinegary taste or smell that develops when a wine is overexposed to air and acquires a trace (or more) of acetic acid.

ACID: One of the taste components of wine. Acidic wine is sometimes described as sour or tart. The taste buds for sensing acidity are found on the sides of the tongue and mouth.

ACIDITY: All wines naturally contain acids that should be in proper balance with fruit and other components. Sufficient acidity gives wine liveliness and crispness, is critical for wines to age, and gives wine thirst-quenching qualities.

AERATING: Letting wine breathe. Aeration occurs upon opening a bottle, by exposing wine to air that can help it develop and mellow, especially red wine.

AFTERTASTE: The aroma and taste that linger at the back of the throat and nose after the wine has been swallowed.

ALCOHOLIC FERMENTATION: Natural, chemical process that turns the sugars of grapes, and any added sugars, into alcohol through the action of yeast. The better sparkling wines undergo a second fermentation in the bottle. This happens because developing bubbles are trapped when the carbon dioxide produced during the fermentation process has nowhere to go.

ALOXE-CORTON (Ah-LOHSS Cor-TONE):   A village in the Côte d'Or in Burgundy, France.

ALSACE: Major wine region in the Northwest of France, noted for its white wines. Alsace borders Germany.

AMONTILLADO: A style of Sherry, amber in color, nutty-tasting, and fairly dry.

APÉRITIF: A before-dinner drink. In theory, it stimulates the appetite (and conversation).

APPELLATION: A specific geographic area. For instance, a Californian wine might be labeled as California or by a progressively more specific area, if applicable—Napa Valley, Napa Valley-Stag's Leap District, or even a single vineyard. (See AVA.)

AROMA: The smell of a wine. Aroma seems to generate a surprising number of adjectives among wine people discussing a beverage made from grape juice.

ASTRINGENCY: A lip-puckering sensation caused by sharp acidity and tannin. A wine's astringent quality often diminishes as the wine ages.

ATTACK: The first impression a wine makes on the palate.

AUSLESE: German white wines made from very ripe, individually selected grape bunches usually affected by *botrytis cinerea*, the "noble rot." These wines tend to be sweet.

AUSTERE: Wine that has very little fruity flavor and high acidity. Some very good wines—French Chablis and Italian Gavi, for instance— may be described as austere.

AVA: An abbreviation for American Viticultural Area. AVAs are U.S. government-approved place-names for wine-producing areas and are used to indicate the wine's place of origin. (See APPELLATION.)

B

BALANCE: Harmony among the wine's components—fruit, acidity, tannins, alcohol.

BARBARESCO (bar-bar-ESS-coh):   A full-bodied DOCG red wine from Piedmont, Italy, made from the Nebbiolo grape and capable of greatness. Barolo and Barbaresco are the top two Nebbiolo-based wines from Piedmont, Italy.

BARBERA (bar-BEAR-ah):   A red grape grown in the Piedmont region. Wines from this grape are growing in popularity because they are affordable and food-friendly. Barbera was once widely planted in California, but many of the vines have been pulled up and replaced by more popular grapes. Barbera grapes are often part of the mix in California red jug wines.

BAROLO (bar-OH-lo):   A full-bodied DOCG red wine from Piedmont, Italy, made from the Nebbiolo grape. Barolo and Barbaresco are the top two Nebbiolo-based wines from Piedmont, Italy.

BEAUJOLAIS (bo-zho-LAY):   A light, fruity red Burgundy wine from the region of Beaujolais, France, made from the Gamay grape.

BEAUJOLAIS NOUVEAU (bo-zho-LAY new-VOH):   The "new" Beaujolais that comes out the third week of November immediately following the harvest.

BIG: Powerful in aroma and flavor; full-bodied wine. Such wines may also be "chewy."

BODY: The weight and texture of a wine. Glycerine is the component of wine most responsible for body.

BORDEAUX: The most important wine region in France, if not the world. The reds from this region are usually blends of Cabernet Sauvignon, Cabernet Franc, and Merlot. White wines are primarily blends of Sauvignon Blanc and Semillon.

BOTRYTIS CINEREA: A mold that affects white wine grapes in certain regions. It helps make them into dessert wines by concentrating the grapes' sugars by reducing their water content. Also known as "noble rot."

BOTTLE AGING: Process of aging a wine in the bottle to help mature and refine its flavors.

BOTTLE FERMENTED: While méthode champenoise sparkling wines could be called "bottle fermented," this term is generally used to pass off transfer-method sparkling wine as being something special. The term "naturally fermented in the bottle" is also used—for which "the bottle" doesn't mean "this bottle." Méthode champenoise is the way superior sparkling wines are made.

BOUQUET: The collection of different aromas from a wine is called its bouquet. It is generally held that a wine is born with aromas, but develops a "bouquet" with bottle age.

BOURGOGNE: The French name for what we call Burgundy, the famous wine region of France, known for its Pinot Noir and Chardonnay.

BREATHING: Exposing wine to air to allow it to complete its evolution before drinking. The wine drinker's term for "aerating."

BRILLIANT: Describes a wine that has a bright, clean appearance, with luminous reflections.

BRIX: Term used to measure the sugar content of grapes prior to harvest. One degree Brix equals 18 grams of dissolved sugar per liter, and Brix measurements in the low twenties are typical for ripe grapes.

BRUT: Term for dry Champagne or sparkling wine. In the Champagne region of France, this term implies only a small amount of added sugar, less than 15 grams per liter.

BULK METHOD: (See CHARMAT METHOD.)

BURGUNDY: The anglicized name of Bourgogne, a major wine region of France. This region is noted for its Chardonnays and Pinot Noirs. It is also a generic name for some red jug wines made in the United States.

BUTTERY: An adjective used to describe wines with a lot of flavor and a smooth texture, referencing the oiliness and flavor of butter. This term more often refers to oak-aged white wines than reds; many Chardonnays and white Burgundies are said to have buttery aromas and flavors. "Almondy" is another adjective that is often used in the same sentence as buttery. The malolactic fermentation is largely responsible for this flavor.

BYOB: Bring your own bottle. This term may be used by a restaurant that does not have a liquor license.

C

CAB: Nickname for Cabernet Sauvignon.

CABERNET: Longer nickname for Cabernet Sauvignon.

CABERNET FRANC: Red-wine grape used primarily as a blending grape. It is popular in France, where it is blended with Cabernet Sauvignon. Château Cheval Blanc, considered by many to be the finest wine from the Saint-Emilion region of France, is usually a blend of 66 percent Cabernet Franc and 34 percent Merlot.

CABERNET SAUVIGNON: Perhaps the noblest of red-wine grapes. Cabernet Sauvignon makes big, complex, and powerful red wines, the greatest of which are very expensive and age gracefully for decades.

CACHET VALUE: The pleasure you get from drinking a trendy or famous wine. Restaurants experience cachet value by having such wines on their menus. The quality aspect of the wine is not part of its cachet value. Dom Pérignon Champagne, for instance, has a lot of cachet value in many social circles. Cachet value may be defined as the pleasure you get from drinking a wine when you know what it is minus the pleasure you would get if you drank it without knowing what it is.

CARAMEL-Y: Used to describe wines, usually white, that have been aged for a long time and have a rich, burnt-sugar flavor. Oak also contributes to this flavor.

CARBONATED WINE: Sparkling wines of inferior quality that have been injected with carbon dioxide, like soft drinks.

CARBONIC MACERATION: Special technique for fermenting young red wines to make them drinkable. Widely used for Beaujolais, this process involves fermenting whole grapes in a carbon dioxide environment, thus preventing oxidation.

CASK: A wooden cask is used to age wine. Casks are many times larger than the standard 55 gallon barrels and thus have less surface area per unit of volume.

CAVA: Spanish sparkling wine made using the Champagne method, undergoing its second fermentation in the same bottle in which it's sold.

CHABLIS (shah-BLEE): Chardonnay-based, somewhat austere white wine from the Chablis district of Burgundy, France.

CHAMPAGNE: A major region of France known for its sparkling wines of the same name. In most countries (but not the United States) this word is not allowed to appear on any bottle of sparkling wine that isn't made in Champagne, France. The Champagne method, or méthode champenoise, was invented in this region.

CHAMPAGNE METHOD: English for méthode champenoise, this is the labor-intensive process by which a second fermentation is created in its bottle resulting in carbonation.

CHAPTALIZATION: The adding of sugar to wine in order to achieve the right alcohol level. Wine grapes grown in cooler climates often don't achieve enough ripeness, thus they lack sufficient sugars to be converted into the desired alcohol level.

CHARACTER: The combination of a wine's features that make it distinguishable from other wines. It is a term usually used as a compliment.

CHARDONNAY: The most popular of all white-wine grapes, and the primary white grape of France's Burgundy region.

CHARMAT METHOD: An inexpensive process for producing huge amounts of sparkling wine. It is also called the "bulk method." Unlike the Champagne method, the second fermentation takes place in a vat, and the resulting product is filtered under pressure into bottles.

CHÂTEAU: A piece of land. For instance, Château Latour is a specific plot of vines in Pauillac, France. This term means the same thing as "domaine." "Domaine" is more frequently used in Burgundy, and "château" is more frequently used in Bordeaux.

CHÂTEAUNEUF-DU-PAPE (shah-toe-NUFF doo PAHP): The name comes from the period of the papal schism (1300s) when French popes summered in the "new castle" near Avignon. It is a district in the southern Rhône region where quality red wine is produced. These wines may be made from up to thirteen different grapes, but Grenache is the primary variety.

CHEWY: A term used to describe red wines with unusual thickness of texture or tannins.

CHIANTI (K'YAHN-tee): A famous red wine made in the Tuscany region of Italy from primarily Sangiovese grapes.

CHIANTI CLASSICO: The core subdistrict of Chianti in Tuscany. There are other subdistricts, the best known of which is Rufina.

CINSAULT: A minor red-wine grape, often used as a blending grape in the Rhône and Languedoc regions of France.

CLARET: Medium-light red wine. In Britain, "claret" is also used to mean red wines from Bordeaux.

CLOSED: Young, undeveloped red wines that do not yet reveal their positive qualities are described as "closed." Breathing can encourage a closed wine to open up.

COMPLEX: A wine with a lot of different flavor and aroma components. Complexity is good.

COOKED: Burnt-fruit flavors resembling raisin. This quality is often found in wines from very hot growing regions.

CORK: Two definitions: 1. the cork that is used to seal the bottle; or 2. an unpleasant smell and/or taste given to a wine by a bad cork (also known as "corked" or "corky").

CORKAGE FEE: If you go to a restaurant that allows you to bring your own wine, the restaurant will often charge a fee. This "corkage fee" covers the cost of having the staff uncork and serve you your wine in the restaurant's wine glasses, which will be cleaned later by restaurant personnel. It also covers some or all of the profits not made on the wine you might have bought had you not brought your own.

CÔTE: A French word for slope, as in the slopes of a river valley. Many vineyards in France are on slopes.

CÔTE D'OR (coat dor):   Literally means "golden slope." A French region that includes the most important Burgundy vineyards.

COUNTRY WINES: France, Italy, and Germany, whose top-quality wines are tightly regulated by their countries' wine laws, also produce light, simple, and inexpensive "country wines." These are known as *vin de pays* in France, *Vino da Tavola* in Italy, and *Tafelwein* in Germany.

COUPAGE: The illicit addition of one wine to another to improve or enhance its qualities.

CRISP: Fresh, brisk character, usually associated with the acidity of white wine.

CRU: French for growth. In French usage, the word means a vineyard of high quality, usually considered worthy of independent recognition under the laws of classification. An officially classified vineyard is a *"cru classé."*

D

DECANTING: Pouring a wine from its bottle into another bottle or container. This allows the wine to breathe, and is also the best way to separate wine from its sediment.

DELICATE: A wine that is light in texture with subtle flavors. Delicate wines are easily overwhelmed by powerfully flavored foods.

DEMI-SEC: A term used to indicate moderately sweet to medium-sweet sparkling wines. It is also used to indicate off-dry versions of Vouvray.

DEVELOPED: Wine that has undergone positive changes during its years of aging. Wines can also develop after a bottle has been opened.

DISTINCTIVE: Elegant, refined character that sets the wine apart.

DOCG/DOC: The abbreviations of Denominazione di Origine Controllata (e Garantita). Of the four tiers of government-regulated Italian wines, DOCG wines are the top rated, and DOC wines make up the second tier. VdT, Vino da Tavola, is the lowest rating for wines shipped abroad, and IGT, Indicazione Geografica Tipica, covers wines outside of the DOCG/DOC laws.

DOMAINE: A specific plot of land. This term means the same thing as "château." "Domaine" is more frequently used in Burgundy, and "château" is more frequently used in Bordeaux.

DOUX: The sweetest of Champagnes.

DRY: Opposite of sweet. By definition, a dry wine has little or no residual sugar left following the fermentation process or processes.

DULL: Lacking flavor and/or enough acidity. Sometimes wines go through a dull phase in their evolutionary process and may emerge as good or even great wines.

DUMB: A wine that doesn't reveal its flavors and aromas. This is because the wine is too young or is served too cold.

E

EARTHY: Smell or flavor reminiscent of earth. European wines are more apt to be earthy than New World wines.

ELEGANT: A wine with flavor, quality, and style that isn't overly heavy, tannic, or acidic. A balance of components is also implied.

EXTRA DRY: Term used on sparkling-wine labels to indicate a wine that is fairly dry, but not as dry as brut.

F

FAT: Full-bodied, low-acid wines are said to be fat.

FERMENTATION: Process in which yeast turns sugar into ethyl alcohol. Heat and carbon dioxide are by-products of this process.

FIGHTING VARIETAL: A class of particularly inexpensive, mass-produced varietal wines. This is a slang term.

FILTERING: The removal of solids and microscopic particulate matter from wine by passing it through a screen.

FINISH: Aftertaste or final impression a wine gives as it leaves your mouth. Long is usually good; short is usually bad.

FINO: The driest, palest style of Sherry.

FIREPLACE WINE: A wine that is as good, if not better, without food than with food. Low acidity, high glycerine content, residual sweetness, moderate-to-low tannin, and fruitiness are characteristics that make for good fireplace wine.

FIRM: Suggests that the elements of a wine's structure are tightly wound together, and it also implies the wine has quite a bit of flavor and structure. "Firm tannins" might indicate a red wine that is well made and has a bright future.

FLESHY: A wine with a lot of big, ripe fruitiness. These wines are thick on the palate. Glycerine can also give a fleshy impression in the mouth.

FLINTY: A dry, mineral-like flavor component that comes from soils containing a lot of limestone. It is an interesting flavor that is an important component of French white wines.

FLOR: A layer of mold that forms in some—but not all—barrels during the Sherry-making process. This development is a good thing. Unfortunately, humans haven't figured out how to make it happen; its formation is still a secret of nature.

FLORAL: A term used to describe the floral scents found in some wines. Riesling is often described as floral.

FLOWERY: See FLORAL.

FLUTE: Special, tall and slender glass for sparkling wines. This is the best shape to keep the carbon dioxide bubbles from vanishing too quickly.

FORTIFIED WINE: Wines with alcohol added. Port, Sherry, Madeira, and Marsala are the major categories of fortified wines.

FORWARD: Prominent, or dominant; a wine is described as "fruit-forward" if it gives a strong, initial fruity impression in the mouth.

FREE RUN: Fermented grape juice obtained not by pressing grapes but rather by letting the juice run freely, thus avoiding the extraction of harsh tannins.

FRESH: A white or rosé wine with a good balance between alcohol and acidity. May also be applied to young red wine.

FRUIT: One of the taste components of wine. The interaction of alcohol and organic acids results in the development of fruit esters. These compounds imitate the flavors and aromas of other fruits.

FRUITY: Refers to prominent fruit flavors and aromas in a wine. Black currants are often referenced in the aromas of Cabernet Sauvignon and Merlot wines, while tropical fruit aromas are found in many Australian Chardonnays.

FULL-BODIED: This term is used to describe a wine with a lot of flavor, alcohol, and thickness that gives a mouth-filling impression in the mouth.

FUMÉ BLANC: A style of Sauvignon Blanc developed in California by Robert Mondavi with the French Pouilly Fumé in mind—dry, smoky, and rich.

G

GAMAY: The red grape variety used to make Beaujolais. Not grown with much success in any other region of the world.

GEWÜRZTRAMINER (geh-VURZ-tra-MEANER):   In German, literally, "spicy Traminer." Grape used for white wines in Alsace and California.

GLYCERINE: A complex alcohol that gives wine its thickness. This is a desirable component, up to a point.

GRAN RESERVA: Name given to Spanish wines that have been aged for a long time, traditionally as much as ten years in oak barrels (American, often) prior to bottling.

GRAND CRU: Literally means "great growth." In France's rating system of Burgundy, this is the top designation of vineyard.

GREEN: Term used to describe a young wine that hasn't developed enough to balance out its acidity.

GRENACHE: A grape that is both workhorse and thoroughbred, grown extensively in the southern Rhône. Known as Garnacha in Spain.

GRIP: A function of tannin. The slightly bitter and dry taste of moderate tannin seems to give the other flavors "traction" in the mouth. Young reds with a lot of tannin may have too much grip.

H

HALBTROCKEN: German for "half-dry." This term is sometimes found on German wine bottles.

HARD: A red wine with tannin showing more than its fruit is often said to be hard. A hard wine may soften with time.

HARMONIOUS: Wines whose elements—fruit, alcohol, acidity, and tannin—are balanced so that no one flavor dominates the others.

HARSH: Rough, biting character from excessive tannin and/or acid. Excessive tannin or acid may be prominent due to a lack of fruit.

HEADY: Strong, aromatic wine with a high concentration of alcohol and other volatile components.

HERBACEOUS: Wines with herbal aromas. Mint, sage, and thyme are three herbs often detected in wine.

HONEST: A relatively flawless but simple wine. It is implied that the wine sells for a fair price.

HYBRID: A cross of two grape varieties of different species, usually a *vitis vinifera* variety and a *vitis riparia* or other native North American variety.

J

JEREZ: The town near the coast of Spain after which Sherry is named.

JOHNSON, HUGH: One of the major wine authorities and author of *The World Atlas of Wine*.

JUG WINE: Inexpensive, unpretentious wine sold in large containers (bottle or bag).

L

LANGUEDOC: A source of good, inexpensive wine (mostly red), located on the Mediterranean coast of France.

LEES: Dead yeast left by the wine after its first fermentation. Sometimes a label will indicate that the wine was allowed to age on its lees before it was clarified and bottled.

LEGS: Traces of oiliness left in the glass by a wine with at least average amounts of alcohol, sugar, and glycerine. The more alcohol, sugar, and glycerine, the bigger the legs. Also known as tears.

LENGTH: A good wine displays its progression of flavors across the palate as you sip it. If this display seems to take a long time, the wine is said to have length.

LIGHT: Refers to a wine that is light in alcohol and/or to its texture and weight in the mouth. Sometimes lightness is desired, and sometimes it is considered a weakness; it depends on the wine. Great Pinot Noirs from Burgundy are often light; great California Cabernet Sauvignons are never light.

LIVELY: A lively wine has a clean aroma and fresh acidity. This term is also used for sparkling wines that have a good amount of carbonation.

LOIRE VALLEY: One of the major regions of France, and the source of Muscadet, Vouvray, Rosé d'Anjou, Chinon, Sancerre, and Pouilly Fumé.

M

MACERATION: The soaking, for a greater or lesser period, of crushed grapes in a fermenting vat.

MADEIRA: An island under Portuguese rule off the coast of Africa, on which the fortified wine by the same name is produced. This fortified wine is usually used more for cooking than drinking.

MAGNUM: A bottle size of 1,500ml rather than the more common 750ml.

MALBEC: A red grape rapidly gaining popularity for its success in Argentina.

MALOLACTIC FERMENTATION: A secondary fermentation that takes place in some white wines and most red wines through bacterial action, whereby the malic acid is converted into lactic acid and the acidity becomes milder.

MANZANILLA: A very dry Sherry style said to have a slightly salty tang acquired during its maturation close to the sea.

MARSALA: A fortified wine produced from local white grapes on the island of Sicily. Available in dry and sweet styles, Marsala is a common ingredient in Italian cooking. Marsala is named after the Sicilian city of the same name.

MATURE: Fully developed, ready-to-drink wine. Ideally, wines are aged until they reach their peak of perfection. Different wines need varying amounts of time to mature. Many great estate wines are crafted to require a decade or more to mature.

MEATY: A wine with a chewy, fleshy fruit, sturdy and firm in structure. This is a wine adjective applied to big red wines such as Cabernet Sauvignon and Zinfandel.

MÉDOC: Bordeaux's largest district, home of the communes of Saint-Julien, Saint-Estèphe, Margaux, and Pauillac.

MELLOW: A wine adjective describing a low-acid wine that is smooth and soft, rather than rough around the edges. Well-made Merlot tends to be a mellow red wine.

MERITAGE: A term coined by California wine producers to indicate a high-quality wine blended from Bordeaux varieties. Because U.S. law requires 75 percent or more of a single grape variety to qualify for varietal labeling, the term "Meritage" was invented to denote a quality wine that doesn't qualify for a varietal designation and would otherwise qualify only for the lowly "table wine" designation.

MERLOT: A red-wine grape whose popularity exploded following the discovery of the "French paradox." Merlot wines tend to be easy-drinking reds and are a big hit with people recently converted to drinking red wine for its health benefits.

MÉTHODE CHAMPENOISE: This translates to the "Champagne Method." The best sparkling wines undergo their second fermentation in the same bottle in which the wine is sold. This laborious process is the méthode champenoise.

MINTY: A desirable aroma in some wines, particularly Cabernet Sauvignon.

MISE EN BOUTEILLE AU CHÂTEAU: This French term translates to "bottled at the estate." This often denotes high quality, as the wine-maker has a personal relationship to the grapes used in crafting a wine.

MOSEL-SAAR-RUWER: A major wine region in Germany that lies along these connected rivers.

MOURVÉDRE: A red grape that rarely stands alone, often used in Rhône and Languedoc blends.

MUSCAT: A type of grape that yields a raisiny fruit-tasting wine. Muscat wines are almost always sweet. Black Muscat makes wines that are dark purple, whereas orange Muscat makes bronze-colored wines.

MUST: The combination of crushed grapes, skins, and pips from which red wine is drawn.

N

NAPA VALLEY: A highly regarded wine region in Northern California where the top U.S. wines are produced. Only 5 percent of California wines come from Napa.

NEBBIOLO: A red grape grown almost exclusively in the Piedmont region of Italy. This is an important red-wine grape, capable of producing great red wines. Unlike Cabernet Sauvignon, which is found on many continents, Nebbiolo is rarely grown with success beyond its home in Piedmont.

NOBLE GRAPES: Grapes that produce the world's finest wines: Cabernet Sauvignon, Pinot Noir, Merlot, Syrah, Nebbiolo, and Sangiovese are noble red grapes, while Chardonnay, Sauvignon Blanc, and Riesling are noble white grapes. There is nothing official about this designation.

NOBLE ROT: This is the nickname for *botrytis cinerea*, a mold that affects certain white grapes and helps make them suitable for dessert wines by concentrating juices and sugars.

NONVINTAGE: A wine made from grapes from more than one harvest.

NOSE: The smell of the wine; it might have a "good nose" or an "off nose."

NOUVEAU: French for "new," this term refers to young wine meant for immediate drinking, as in Beaujolais Nouveau, which may have been made only weeks before it is consumed.

NUTTY: Nutlike aromas and flavors that develop in certain wines such as Sherries or old white wines.

O

OAK: Smell and taste, rather vanilla-like, imparted on a wine by oak barrels. Oak is a very popular tool of the winemaker, and sometimes it is overused. Oak flavor is occasionally added via oak chips thrown into the vat.

OENOLOGY: The study of wine.

OENOPHILE: One who loves, appreciates, and studies wine.

OFF-DRY: Wine with noticeable residual sugar, usually above 1 percent by volume.

OLOROSO: A dark Sherry that may be sweet or dry. The sweet versions are usually called "cream" or "brown" Sherry.

OXIDATION: An alteration wines undergo after exposure to oxygen. Some exposure to oxygen is good for the wine and its flavors. Eventually, however, oxygen helps turn wine into vinegar and other aromatic compounds, such as acetaldahyde and ethyl acetate.

P

PALE: Used to describe wines with less color than similar-styled wines.

PALE DRY: The style in which Fino Sherry is made.

PALOMINO: The primary white grape used to make Sherry.

PARKER, ROBERT: One of the major wine authorities and publisher of *The Wine Advocate*.

PEPPERY: Red wine that has a hint of black pepper flavor, such as Zinfandel, is said to be peppery.

PETITE SIRAH: Another name for the mystery grape that was mistakenly brought to the United States instead of the Syrah grape. In Californian heat and sunshine, Petite Sirah produces deeply colored and flavored wines.

PHYLLOXERA: A vine louse that kills *vinifera* vines.

PIEDMONT: The great wine region of Northern Italy, famous for its Nebbiolo, Barbera, and Dolcetto wines.

PINOTAGE: Unique to South Africa, this grape is a cross between the Pinot Noir and Cinsault grapes.

PINOT BLANC: A reliable white-wine grape, known as Pinot Bianco in Italy. This grape is used to make simple and clean wines in Italy, Alsace, and California.

PINOT GRIGIO: White-wine grape, also known as Pinot Gris. This grape produces good white wine in Italy, Alsace, and Oregon.

PINOT NOIR: The noble red grape of Burgundy and the West Coast of the United States. This grape isn't easy to grow, but it produces wonderful light- and medium-bodied wines that have enthralled connoisseurs for centuries.

PIPS: Grape seeds. Pips are a source of tannin in red wine.

PORT: Fortified red wine from the Douro Valley of Portugal, where it is known as Porto. This class of wine is available in a variety of styles, including Ruby, Tawny, and Vintage.

POUILLY-FUISSÉ (POO-yee FWEE-say): Hugely popular French white wine, made from Chardonnay grapes in the commune of Fuissé (or one of four other neighboring communes) in the Mâcon subregion of Burgundy.

PREMIER CRU: Literally meaning "first growth," this designation indicates the highest level of quality in Médoc, Bordeaux, but it is the second-highest level behind *grand cru* in Burgundy.

PRICKLE: Presence of tiny natural bubbles in some young wines.

PROVENCE: A minor wine-producing region of France, often lumped together with the neighboring Rhône region. Provence is best known for high-quality, dry rosé wines.

PUNT: The indentation in the bottom of many wine bottles.

Q

QUALITÄTSWEIN BESTIMMTER ANBAUGEBIETE (QbA): The middle quality of German wine. (See QUALITÄTSWEIN MIT PRÄDIKAT.)

QUALITÄTSWEIN MIT PRÄDIKAT (QmP): The highest quality level of German wines. The "prädikats" are the designation of sugar content at harvest. From driest to sweetest, they are Kabinett, Spätlese,

Auslese, Beerenauslese, Trockenbeerenauslese, and Eiswein. QmP wines may not have any sugar added to them. The second-highest quality category of German wine, QbA, includes well-made wines with more general regional designations. Tafelwein, rarely exported to the United States, is the lowest level.

R

RAISINY: Smells reminiscent of raisin, found in wines made from very ripe or overripe grapes. Australian red wines are often raisiny. Muscat wines are inherently raisiny, regardless of the ripeness of the harvested Muscat grapes.

REGION: A large subdivision of a wine-producing country. For instance, France has seven major regions: Bordeaux, Burgundy, Rhône, Loire, Champagne, Languedoc, and Alsace.

RESERVA: This word on a Spanish wine label indicates that the wine has been aged in a barrel and/or a bottle longer than regular wines from the same region. *Riserva* with an "i" is the Italian equivalent.

RESERVE: This term has no legal definition in the United States. Reserve wines are implied to be aged longer and better-made than regular bottlings.

RHÔNE VALLEY: Region in France noted for big, strong reds and some interesting white wines.

RICH: An adjective used to describe a wine that has a lot of flavor, body, and aroma.

RIESLING: A noble white wine grape that is more popular in Europe than North America. The best of these wines come from Germany, Austria, and Alsace.

RIOJA: A wine region in Northern Spain where the local Tempranillo grape is often blended with a little Garnacha to make red wines bearing the name Rioja. Some white Rioja is also produced, from the Viura grape.

ROBUST: Full-bodied, full-flavored, and high in alcohol.

ROSÉ: Pink-colored wine, usually made from red-wine grapes fermented with minimal contact with grape skins, which produces a lighter color. Some rosés are made from mixing a small amount of red wine with white. White Zinfandel is a rosé made from the red Zinfandel grape. Many but not all rosés are noticeably sweet.

ROSE D'ANJOU: A rosé wine from the Loire Valley in France, made from Cabernet Franc, Cabernet Sauvignon, and other red grapes.

ROUGH: Describes a wine with harsh edges that is biting and sometimes unpleasant. Rough wines are sometimes a good match with garlic.

ROUND: Describes a wine with balance and harmony among its various components—fruitiness, acidity, alcohol, tannin, glycerine, and sweetness—that literally gives a three-dimensional, round impression in the mouth.

S

SAINT-EMILION: A major subregion of Bordeaux, France.

SANGIOVESE: A red-wine grape grown mainly in Italy. It is the primary grape in Chianti.

SANGRIA: A wine drink that is served chilled. It is made from wine and fruit.

SAUTERNES: An important subregion of Bordeaux, France, famous for dessert wines of the same name.

SAUVIGNON BLANC: Generally a notch below Riesling and Chardonnay in terms of the high end of the wine spectrum, this white grape makes some excellent food wines. Goat cheese seems to be Sauvignon Blanc's match made in heaven.

SCREWPULL: An ingenious device for extracting corks from bottles.

SEC: Literally means "dry." However, in terms of Champagne, it actually means noticeably sweet.

SECOND-LABEL WINE: Many top producers in France, California, and elsewhere maintain the quality of their flagship wines by declassifying less-than-perfect lots of wine and bottling them as second-label wines. In bad years, these producers may declassify an entire vintage.

SEDIMENT: The material found at the bottom of a bottle of red wine, which comes from the wine itself.

SEMILLON: A white-wine grape often used in France as a blending grape with Sauvignon Blanc, and as a soloist in the U.S. and Australia. It is also commonly used for making dessert wines.

SHARP: A wine with prominent, forward acidity is said to be sharp. Sharp wines can "cut through" rich, creamy sauces.

SHERRY: A type of fortified wine from Spain. Sherries can be sweet or not, heavy or light in body, and dark or light in color.

SHIRAZ: The Iranian city where the red-wine grape Syrah supposedly originated. Winemakers in Australia and South Africa—and sometimes California—refer to the Syrah as Shiraz. This grape makes some interesting and affordable red wines.

SHORT: Refers to when the finish, or aftertaste, of a wine ends abruptly.

SILKY: An adjective describing wines with a smooth texture and finish. Glycerine is the component most closely related to silkiness. "Silky" is not very different from "velvety." Excessive tannin prevents a wine from appearing silky.

SIMPLE: Opposite of complex. Straightforward, inexpensive wines are often referred to as being simple. It is not a negative term when describing a $7 bottle of wine, but is a criticism of a $70 bottle.

SMOKY: An aroma sometimes associated with Sauvignon Blanc and Pinot Noir.

SMOOTH: Describes a wine somewhat rich in glycerine and usually light in tannin and acidity, which feels good in the mouth.

SOAVE: The name of a white-wine-producing district of Veneto, Italy.

SOFT: May refer to soft, gentle fruit in delicate wines, or to a lack of acidity in wines without proper structure. It is used on a label occasionally to indicate a low alcohol content.

SOLERA: The aging system used for Sherry, where old and new barrels are connected in such a way that blends multiple vintages, sometimes going back a century.

SOMMELIER: A restaurant employee who purchases wine for the establishment and assists customers wishing to order wine. A broad knowledge of matching food and wine is essential for this job.

SONOMA VALLEY: Northern Californian wine region, larger and more diverse than neighboring Napa Valley.

SPANNA: Local name in Northern Italy for Nebbiolo grapes.

SPARKLING WINE: Wines with bubbles created by trapped carbon dioxide gas, induced by a second, enclosed fermentation.

SPICY: Having the character or aroma of spices such as clove, mint, cinnamon, or pepper. Gewürztraminer and Zinfandel are noted for their spiciness.

SPUMANTE: Italian for sparkling wine.

STEELY: Usually applied to white wines that are firmly structured with taut balance tending toward high acidity.

STEMMY: Indicates a harsh, green, tannic flavor, perhaps drawn from the stems of the grapes.

STRAW: Used to describe a white wine with a deep golden color, like straw.

STRAWBERRY: A fruity aroma that appears in certain red or rosé wines.

STRUCTURE: The framework of the wine, made up of its acid, alcohol, and tannin content. Great wines must have a good underlying structure to support the other flavor components, such as fruitiness.

SULFITES: Both naturally occurring and added to wines, they are used as a defense against oxidation and bacterial spoilage prior to fermentation.

SUPER-TUSCAN: High quality, non-DOC/G red wines, often made with Cabernet Sauvignon.

SWEET: Usually indicates the presence of residual sugar, retained when grape sugar is not completely converted to alcohol. Even dry wines, however, may have an aroma of sweetness, the combination of intense fruit or ripeness. Sweetness may be considered a flaw if not properly balanced with acidity.

SYLVANER: A workhorse white grape of Germany, often blended with Riesling. It is commonly found in QbA wine such as Liebfraumilch.

SYRAH: Known as Shiraz in Australia and South Africa, this red grape is used to make some great wines and some great-value wines. While the Northern Rhône of France has long been a source for good Syrah, great versions are coming from California, Tuscany, Chile, Australia, and South Africa.

T

TANNIN: A natural component found to varying degrees in the skins, seeds, and stems of grapes as well as oak barrels. It is most prominent in red wines, where it creates a dry, puckering sensation in young reds. Tannin softens with aging and is a major component in the structure of red wines.

TART: A sharp taste that comes from a wine's natural acidity. Not necessarily a negative term.

TARTARIC ACID: The predominant wine acid that occurs naturally in grapes.

TEARS: Traces of oiliness left in the glass by a wine with at least average amounts of alcohol, sugar, and glycerine. The more alcohol, sugar, and glycerine, the bigger the tears. Also known as legs.

TEMPRANILLO: The major red grape of Spain's Rioja and Ribera del Duero regions. Tempranillo, also known as Tinto Fino, is not widely cultivated beyond Spain's borders.

TERROIR: A French word that refers to the influence of soil and climate, rather than grape variety, on winemaking.

THIN: A negative term for a wine (usually red) with insufficient body, flavor, and/or color.

TINTO: This is Spanish for red wine.

TIRED: A wine that is past its peak of flavor development. Such a wine should have been opened at an earlier time.

TOBACCO: An aroma that is noticeable in some mature wines. This is considered to be a good thing, especially in Bordeaux or Californian Cabernet Sauvignon.

TROCKEN: German for "dry." German winemakers use this term to combat their reputation for producing mostly sweet wines.

TUSCANY: One of the major wine regions of Italy, it is the home of Chianti and Brunello di Montalcino.

U

UNCTUOUS: An adjective to describe a thick, rich, and glycerine-laden wine with an equally rich aroma.

V

VANILLA: A spicy aroma and flavor imparted to a wine by oak-aging.

VARIETAL: Wine that is made from one dominant grape variety and is labeled as such is a varietal wine.

VARIETAL CORRECTNESS: A wine that exhibits the signature characteristics of the grape variety with which it is labeled is considered to be varietally correct. Many cheaper varietals are not varietally correct, although they might taste good.

VARIETY: Type of grape within the species *Vitis vinifera*.

VELVETY: A wine that is smooth and silky in texture is often called velvety. This is a signature characteristic of American Pinot Noir. Low acid, low tannin, and generous glycerine make for a velvety wine.

VIN: French for "wine."

VINEGAR: Wine turns into vinegar when aerobic acetobacter convert ethyl alcohol into acetic acid. Unlike tartaric or other wine acids, acetic acid is volatile, i.e., you can smell it.

VINIFICATION: The process of winemaking from harvest to bottling is called vinification.

VINO: Spanish and Italian for "wine."

VINTAGE: The year in which the wine was harvested. This information should appear on the bottle.

VINTNER: Another term for winemaker, the person who actually controls the equipment and makes the decisions in the production of wine.

VIOGNIER: A white grape that does well in the Rhône, with apricot-like fruit flavors.

W

WHITE ZINFANDEL: A rosé made from the red-wine Zinfandel grape.

WINE ADVOCATE: Robert Parker's newsletter about wine, targeted toward wine enthusiasts. Reviews in this magazine have a powerful impact on the wine market. *The Wine Advocate* does not accept advertising and therefore presents itself as unbiased.

WINE SPECTATOR: A flashy magazine about wine, with many columnists, articles, and tasting notes. Although *Wine Spectator* accepts advertising from wineries, its reviews are considered to be reliable.

WINE STEWARD: (See SOMMELIER.)

WOODY: A wine that shows prominent wood flavors and aromas, or has absorbed too much oak flavor from casks or barrels, is described as woody. However, some wood is good, because it adds complexity to wine.

Y

YEAST: Single-cell organisms that thrive on the grape skin that facilitate the alcohol-fermentation process. Some winemakers use specific strains of yeast, while others rely on naturally occurring, wild yeast.

YEASTY: A bready smell, sometimes detected in wines that have undergone secondary fermentation, such as Champagne. This can be used as either a positive or negative adjective.

Z

ZINFANDEL: Red-wine grape that thrives in Californian heat and sunshine. White Zinfandel is a rosé, made from the red-wine Zinfandel grape.

Index

A

Abruzzo, 154–55
aging, 55–56, 68, 212–13
Alsace, 149–50
Amarone, 158
Appellation d'Origine Contrôlée
    (AOC) laws, 11, 142
Apulia, 154
Argentina, 176–77
Arneis, 159
Asti Spumante, 159
Australia, 180–82
Austria, 168–70

B

Barbera, 117–18
Bardolino, 158
barrels, 6, 47, 55–56, 68
Beaujolais, 112–13, 146, 147
Blanc de Blancs, 151
Blanc de Noirs, 151
Bordeaux, 141, 143–45
Bourgogne. See Burgundy
Brachetto d'Aqui, 160
brandy, 26–27, 237
bretty wines, 79
Brut Rosé, 151
Burgundy, 62, 141, 145–47

C

Cabernet Franc, 116–17
Cabernet Sauvignon, 56–57, 91–94, 141

Calabria, 154
California, 7–14, 170–73
Campania, 154
Carmènere, 177–78
Catalonia, 166
centrifuging, 42
Chablis, 61–62, 146
Champagne, 18–21, 25–26, 141,
    150–52
chaptalization, 45
Chardonnay, 57, 119–22, 141,
    229–30
Chenin Blanc, 127–29, 141
Chianti, 62, 155–56
Chile, 177–78
clarification process, 80–81
climate, 138–39
cold stabilization, 43
complexity, 70–71
Concord grape, 89–90
cooking wines, 235–37
corkage fees, 221
cork taint, 78
Côte de Beaune, 141, 146–47
Côte de Nuits, 146

D

dessert wines, 21–26

E

economic factors, 187–93
eiswein (ice wine), 23–24, 163

entertaining, 204–9
Epicurious, 241

F

fermentation, 40, 45–46
fighting varietals, 62–63
filtration, 42
fining, 41–42
fizziness, 79–80
flaws, 73–81
food pairings: with Barbera, 118; with
    Cabernet Sauvignon, 94; with
    Chardonnay, 121; with Chenin
    Blanc, 128; with Gamay, 113; with
    Gewürztraminer, 135; with
    Grenache, 110; with Grüner
    Veltliner, 136; guidelines for,
    223–33; with Malbec, 115; with
    Merlot, 99; with Nebblio, 106;
    with Pinot Blanc, 130; with Pinot
    Grigio, 134; with Pinot Noir, 96;
    with Riesling, 125; with Rioja, 114;
    with Sangiovese, 108–9; with
    Sauvignon Blanc, 123; with
    Syrah/Shiraz, 101; with Viognier,
    132; with White Zinfandel, 104;
    with Zinfandel, 104
fortified wines, 26–35
France, 140–52
French cuisine, 225–26
Friuli, 157

G

Gamay, 111–13
Gavi, 159
geographic origins, 85–88, 142; See also
    specific regions
Germany, 161–64
Gewürztraminer, 134–35
glassware, 206, 207–8

grapes: See also specific varieties; ideal
    conditions for, 138–40; quality of,
    56–58
Grenache, 110–13
Grüner Veltliner, 136

H

handcrafted wines, 64
Haut-Médoc, 141
health benefits, viii, 13
house wine, 209–10

I

Italy, 152–61

J

jug wines, 61–62
juices, 67–68

K

kosher wine, 35–37

L

labels, 85–88, 142–43, 160, 162–64
laws, regulating wine industry, 11, 86,
    142
Loire, 141, 149

M

macroclimates, 140
Madeira, 33–34, 236
Malbec, 115–16, 176
Marsala, 34–35, 236–37
meat dishes, 231–32
Médoc, 144–45
Merlot, 13–14, 97–100, 141
microclimates, 140
midrange varietals, 63
Moscato d'Asti, 159–60
Muscadet, 141, 149

N

Napa Valley, 172
Nebbiolo, 105–7, 159
New York, 175–76
New Zealand, 182–83

O

oak barrels, 6, 47, 55–56, 68
Oregon, 173–75
oxidation, 40–41, 78–79

P

Pacific Northwest, 173–75
Parker, Robert, 242–43
pasta dishes, 233
Petite Sirah, 101, 102
phylloxera louse, 8–9, 89, 165–66
Piedmont, 158–60
Pinotage, 179
Pinot Blanc, 129–30
Pinot Grigio/Pinot Gris, 133–34, 174–75
Pinot Noir, 57, 95–97, 141, 174
Port, 27–30, 168, 236
Portugal, 167–68
Pouilly-Fumé, 149
poultry, 231
Priorato, 166
Prohibition, 9–10
Prosecco, 157
Provence, 141

Q

quality spectrum, 61–71

R

racking, 42
red meat, 231
red wine: *See also specific varieties*; for cooking, 236; with fish, 227–28, 230; production of, 43–44, 47–50; table, 16–17
regional wineries, 244–46
reserve wines, 64
restaurant wines, 192–93, 215–22
Rhine, 62
Rhône, 147–48
Ribero Duero, 167
Riesling, 57, 124–26, 161–62, 164
Rioja, 113–14, 165–66
Romans, 5–6
Rosé d'Anjou, 149
rosé wine, 17–18, 141, 149

S

Sancerre, 149
Sangiovese, 107–9
Sardinia, 153
Sauternes, 141
Sauvignon Blanc, 122–24, 141, 182
seafood, 232
sediment, 81
Sekt, 164
Semillon, 130–31
Sherry, 30–33, 165, 236
Shiraz. *See* Syrah/Shiraz
Sicily, 153
Soave, 158
soil conditions, 139–40
Sonoma Valley, 172
South Africa, 178–79
Spain, 165–67
sparkling wine, 18–21, 25–26, 164, 237; *See also* Champagne
super-Tuscans, 156
Syrah/Shiraz, 100–2

T

table wine, 15–18
tannins, 48

temperature, 77
Tempranillo, 113–14
Téte de Cuvée, 152
Trentino-Alto Adige, 157
Tuscany, 155–56

U

Umbria, 155
unfiltered wines, 76
United States, 170–76

V

Valpolicella, 158
varietal correctness, 91
varietal labeling, 86–87
varietals, 62–63
Veneto, 157–58
Vermouth, 237
vin de pays, 143
vines, age of, 67
Vine Times, 242
vineyards, 67
Vins De'limités de Qualité Supérieure
    (VDQS), 143
vintages, 64–66, 152, 202
Viognier, 131–33
Vitis vinifera, 89, 90
Vouvray, 149

W

Washington, 173–74
Web sites, 241–46
weddings, 205–6
white wine: See also specific varieties;
    with beef, 228, 229–30; for cooking,
    235; production of, 43–47; table, 16
White Zinfandel, 13, 103–4

wine: See also specific varieties;
    choosing, 203–4, 209–10, 224–33;
    cooking with, 235–37; economics
    of, 187–93; for entertaining, 204–9;
    expensive, 66–71; food and. See
    food pairings; history of, vii–viii,
    3–14; old, 83–74; out of balance,
    76; poorly made, 75–76; qualities of
    good, 53–59, 66–71; in restaurants,
    192–93, 215–22; shopping for,
    195–213; types of, 15–37; without
    food, 233–34; young, 74–75
Wine.com, 243
wine acids, viii
wine cellars, 210–13
wine distribution, 201–3
Wine Enthusiast, 243
wine futures, 213
wine industry, 7–14
Wine Institute, 244
WineLinx.com, 244
Wine Lover's Page, 242
winemaking, 5–9, 39–50; clarification
    process, 41–43; costs of, 190–91;
    oxidation and, 40–41; of red wine,
    43–44, 47–50; of white wine, 43–47
wineries, regional, 244–46
Wine Searcher, 243
Wine Spectator, 242
wine stores, 187–90, 195–204
Wine Tool, The, 242

Z

Zinfandel, 103–5